Sharing Books
TALKING SCIENCE

Valerie Bang-Jensen · Mark Lubkowitz   FOREWORD BY LESTER LAMINACK

Sharing Books
TALKING SCIENCE
·······
Exploring Scientific Concepts with Children's Literature

HEINEMANN
Portsmouth, NH

Heinemann
361 Hanover Street
Portsmouth, NH 03801–3912
www.heinemann.com

Offices and agents throughout the world

> *The authors have dedicated a great deal of time and effort to writing the content of this book, and their written expression is protected by copyright law. We respectfully ask that you do not adapt, reuse, or copy anything on third-party (whether for-profit or not-for-profit) lesson-sharing websites. As always, we're happy to answer any questions you may have.*
>
> **—Heinemann Publishers**

The authors and publisher wish to thank those who have generously given permission to reprint borrowed material:

NGSS Crosscutting Concepts, pages 3–5: Next Generation Science Standards is a registered trademark of Achieve. Neither Achieve nor the lead states and partners that developed the Next Generation Science Standards was involved in the production of, and does not endorse, this product.

Excerpts from "Fossil" in *Forest Has a Song* by Amy Ludwig VanDerwater. Copyright © 2013 by Amy Ludwig VanDerwater. Published by Clarion Books, an imprint of Houghton Mifflin Harcourt Publishing Company. Reprinted with permission from the publisher.

Library of Congress Cataloging-in-Publication Data
Names: Bang-Jensen, Valerie, author. | Lubkowitz, Mark, author.
Title: Sharing books, talking science : exploring scientific concepts with
    children's literature / Valerie Bang-Jensen and Mark Lubkowitz.
Description: Portsmouth, NH : Heinemann, [2017] | Includes bibliographical references.
Identifiers: LCCN 2016044776 | ISBN 9780325087740
Subjects: LCSH: Science—Study and teaching (Elementary). | Literature and science.
Classification: LCC LB1585 .B26 2017 | DDC 372.35/044—dc23

LC record available at https://lccn.loc.gov/2016044776

Editor: Katie Wood Ray
Production: Vicki Kasabian
Interior and cover designs: Suzanne Heiser
Cover image: books © Getty Images Prestige/Holloway
Typesetter: Kim Arney
Manufacturing: Steve Bernier

Printed in the United States of America on acid-free paper
21 20 19 18   PAH   2 3 4 5

This one's for our kids:

Bree and Nell, and Jax and Zander.

CONTENTS

Foreword by Lester Laminack   viii

Acknowledgments   x

1   Exploring Scientific Concepts with Children's Literature   1

2   Pattern: The Superhero of Science   11

3   Cause and Effect: Making Ripples   29

4   Structure and Function: Appreciating the Paper Clip   42

5   Scale, Proportion, and Quantity: The Goldilocks Scale   58

6   Systems and System Models: Life in a Fishbowl   75

7   Energy and Matter: Let's Get the Ball Rolling   92

8   Stability and Change: What's the New Normal?   108

Afterword Are You Ready for the Championship of Crosscutting Concepts?   123
        It Takes Place at Recess!

Children's Literature Cited   125

FOREWORD

I marvel at folks who can take something complex and present it as if it were common sense. I stand back and study how they break it down and present it in a manner that leaves me thinking, *How come I didn't think of this?* That is exactly how I felt by the time I reached the end of the first chapter in this book. And on the last page I would have given Valerie and Mark a standing ovation had I been in their audience. This work is smart yet they make it so very accessible.

Perhaps it is the pairing of an education professor and a biology professor as coauthors that brings this particular focus and wisdom to the page. Clearly it works to merge the passion for literature and the passion for science into a passion for teaching. The current attention given to STEM/STEAM has many of us exploring new ways to make science more accessible, more practical, more inviting to our students, and less intimidating for ourselves. Mark and Valerie have given us a new tool to do just that. Together they provide us with a lens for noticing science everywhere, and most happily, in the pages of many of our favorite picture books. There are the expected titles with a science focus, and you'll be pleased to find many of the recommended authors' names printed on the spines in your nonfiction collection. But you'll be surprised when they gently lead you to notice how the principles of science and the seven crosscutting concepts can be found in the plots and structures of some of your favorite fiction. It is amazing what you see when you are wearing different glasses.

Valerie and Mark show us how to notice and name pattern, cause and effect, structure and function, scale, systems and system models, energy and matter, and stability and change in a variety of genres. Along the way they help us recognize how these seven crosscutting concepts overlap and weave a broader and deeper understanding of the world. As you proceed through the book you will find yourself developing what they refer to as a *scientific habit of mind*. Those of us who live our lives in the reading–writing world are familiar with the idea of "living a writerly life." We naturally approach a text with a reader lens or a writer lens. In this book Mark and Valerie nudge us to live a scientific life: to think like a scientist, talk like a scientist, and read like a scientist so that we question the texts we encounter and come to notice what has been there all along. They give us a new way to revisit texts for different purposes and, as with anything, this emerging awareness brings life into focus in new and interesting ways. We get a fresh look at science while we develop the schema necessary for organizing our learning and building the vocabulary that will enable us to communicate our insights, formulate our questions, and develop deeper conceptual understandings.

Read-aloud sessions have been given much more attention in recent years. We have come to recognize the power of bringing children into the flock of readers with brilliant models of literature delivered on the cadence of a well-practiced voice. We have seen the power of sharing books and visiting them again and again as we lift ideas, vocabulary, and craft to the surface for our students to notice and learn to employ on their own. I celebrate that attention to literature and to the seemingly magic power of read-aloud experiences. Now we have another powerful reason to read aloud to children across the grades and throughout the curriculum. Valerie and Mark have merged their worlds of literature and science into a practical, accessible, commonsense tool for the rest of us.

—Lester Laminack

ACKNOWLEDGMENTS

If there's one person who made this book hum, it's Zander Lubkowitz, the kid who was always ready with a quotable observation, illustrations that spoke better than our words, and a knack for helping us see how kids can think like a scientist. We too want to visit Zandronia.

Teachers rock. Several were kind enough to read our chapters in progress, create lessons from the book, and were brave enough to let us see our ideas in action. We loved listening to the many astute observations in class discussions and feel honored to feature some of their students' voices and pictures in these pages. Thank you: Rebecca Haslam, Barb Aiken, Callie Lumbra, Carole Carlson, Shannon Roesch, Colleen Cowell, Matt Hajdun, Betsy Patrick, and students in Valerie's Making Meaning course—you know who you are. An early meeting over a robust cup of coffee with Christian Courtemanche helped us get friendly with the crosscutting concepts. And at the other end of the project, Caroline Crawford provided grist for the title mill. We owe a special note of thanks to Elyse Gentile for nailing the comparison words *shout* and *whisper* that made the literature section sing.

Colleagues from the Saint Michael's College Biology, Physics, Math, and Education Departments were always on call for hallway help. Shout-outs in particular to Donna Bozzone, John O'Meara, Alain Brizard, Tim Whiteford, and Mary Beth Doyle for insightful conversations. We relied on Kristen Hindes, librarian superhero, for her superpower of always finding a book that was just right. We appreciate the opportunity that Saint Michael's offered us in the form of a sabbatical to tackle this book.

Family and friends indulged us in numerous discussions about the concepts at the breakfast table and on bike rides, car trips, and beach walks. Although we know that scale is relative, we can never thank you enough: Ginger Lubkowitz, Lars Bang-Jensen, Judith Bree, Alison Blay-Palmer, Walter Palmer, Travis Bouker, Julie Campoli, and Valerie's chorus carpool.

We will forever be grateful to Katie Wood Ray to whom we still owe a Heady Topper and a homemade taco dinner for being everything we could ever hope for in an editor and more. Her vision, humor, and tact provided this project with both its structure and function. She believed in our project from the beginning and her insight and expectations made our book the best it could be—thank you (and we got in one last em dash).

*To think like a scientist is to remember
that a system is stable, changing, or both,
depending upon scale.*

1

EXPLORING SCIENTIFIC CONCEPTS WITH CHILDREN'S LITERATURE

After lunch, Callie has settled her class of second and third graders onto the rug for the next chapter of *Charlotte's Web*. Monique is sitting cross-legged, elbows on knees, resting her chin in her hands, enraptured by the story. Alejandro reclines, gazing contemplatively at the ceiling, while Bree wiggles her leg, listening intently. As Callie reads a passage describing Charlotte's weaving technique, Wiley sits up and proclaims, "That web won't catch flies. She's not using the sticky thread."

Prompted by Wiley's observation, Callie seizes the opportunity to make a connection to science and replies, "What a smart observation. Let's hear that again." She rereads: "A spider can produce several kinds of thread. She uses a dry, tough thread for foundation lines, and she uses a sticky thread for snare lines—the ones that catch and hold insects. Charlotte decided to use her dry thread for writing the new message." Callie asks the class, "How is this web different from Charlotte's usual webs? What is it for? What's its *function*?"

Hayley volunteers that this web is for messages, not for catching flies, and Callie responds, "Yes, this web has a different function." Hansi says, "Charlotte doesn't need sticky thread to spell a word," and Juniper adds, "If she used the sticky thread she might catch a big bug that would mess up the word."

"That's right," replies Callie, teaching into the idea. "This web has a different structure because it has a different function."

After Wiley noticed the structure and function relationship, Callie then named the concept for the class, slowing down the discussion to explore it further. In only a few moments, this scientific concept became clearer as the students realized how Charlotte manipulates structure and function in her web to save her friend Wilbur. Now that the idea is in the classroom, Callie can continue this discussion any time a web or other structure appears in the book. Her teacher thinking is, *How could we keep this conversation going and deepen it across the rest of this book, into the classroom, and even the world?* And at any time in the future, Callie may decide to build upon these discussions during read-aloud. If she's sharing *Jack and the Beanstalk,* for example, she might ask, "What is it about the structure of this beanstalk that allows Jack to climb so high?" Through conversations like this, she knows it won't be long before her students are seeing structure and function everywhere.

Although Callie couldn't have anticipated Wiley's comment about Charlotte's web, she was poised to make a responsive teaching decision because she now has the understanding and language for discussing scientific concepts. She has learned to "hear and see the science" in what her students say, do, and think, and she has learned the right questions to help them understand important concepts—she has developed a habit of mind for thinking like a scientist. For example, if her students notice that Jack's giant makes the golden goose look really small, Callie knows they are hinting at scale and proportion and she may decide to launch a discussion about another key concept. This book will help you develop this same mindset for creating teachable moments where you and your students can explore the crosscutting concepts of science when you're sharing children's literature. Books offer many opportunities to make connections to these concepts, and by calling attention to them, you will help your students see that science really is a part of everything that is happening around us.

A Scientific Habit of Mind

Make a mental list of all of the things you heard in the news in the last week that scientists are studying. Our list includes: cancer, climate, Zika virus, glacier waterfalls, self-driving cars, kinetic weaponry, drones, goat stomachs, and La Niña. What do people who study such wildly different things have in common? In other words, what makes a scientist a scientist? In laboratories and field stations across the world, scientists follow basically the same practices (the scientific method) and ways of thinking about whatever it is they are studying. They share a habit of mind. In fact, a few basic concepts guide the work of scientists in every field. To develop a scientific habit of mind, your students will need to build a schema for seeing the world through the lens of the seven crosscutting concepts described in the Next Generation Science Standards (NGSS).

The seven crosscutting concepts are:

pattern

cause and effect

structure and function

scale

systems and system models

energy and matter

stability and change.

These concepts form a scientific habit of mind and are arguably the most substantive innovation in current science curriculum. No matter how your science curriculum changes, these concepts are like gravity; they are never going away.

Because they share a common framework for thinking about science, someone studying goat stomachs can converse intelligently with someone studying La Niña. They may have different knowledge bases, but they use the same framework for thinking about their respective topics. The goat researcher knows all about physiology, diet, and microbes, and the meteorologist delves into thermodynamics and water chemistry. Both perform experiments to answer their research questions. So how do they communicate meaningfully? This is where we can see the importance of the crosscutting concepts. These seven ideas form a conceptual mindset and common language for thinking like a scientist. That's why the meteorologist might ask the goat researcher a question like, "What *patterns* did you notice when the diet changed and what do you think is the *cause*?" Because the two scientists share a habit of mind and its language, even if their content and experimental approaches are different, the meteorologist knows how to frame a meaningful question that the goat researcher will know how to respond to. Most of us, like Callie, are not scientists by training, but all of us can develop the mindset once we understand these concepts. This is why we wrote this book: to help teachers and their students develop the conceptual framework for thinking, talking, and reading like scientists.

Reading Like a Scientist

The idea for this book formed serendipitously when Valerie invited Mark to attend her graduate education class about nonfiction. Both had recently joined the faculty at Saint Michael's College, Mark in the Biology Department and Valerie in the Education Department. Valerie wanted to explore with her class how our own education and experiences shape the way we respond to a text. When Mark asked how he should prepare, Valerie said, "Just bring your science brain."

Valerie read *Winter Barn* (Parnall) aloud and invited her students to respond. Being seasoned teachers, they jumped right in by commenting thoughtfully on the quiet mood created by the sparse pen and ink drawings of the weathered barn in the snow, the rhythm of the season, and the poetic and accurate text. They described the farm animals overwintering in their cozy stalls and wilder animals, like snakes, mice, and porcupines that sought refuge in the cracks and crevices of the stone foundation. When it was Mark's turn to comment on the book, he emphatically proclaimed, "It's a horror story! It's about predators and prey entering the same system (the barn) to try to survive the winter by competing for space and resources." This response, of course, was why Valerie invited Mark to her class in the first place—to show that our lenses shape how we interpret stories, events, and even our lives. (Note: The original idea for looking at *Winter Barn* with the lens of a scientist comes from Benedict and Carlisle [1992].)

As this anecdote shows, there are many ways to view the world; it is sort of like owning a collection of different eye glasses. One day we may choose our sunglasses, and on another, our reading glasses, rose-colored glasses, or X-ray glasses, each for a different purpose. Just as we can metaphorically alter the way we see the world by swapping out our glasses, we can literally change the way we understand the world by developing a scientific lens.

Watch how this mindset shaped Mark's response to *Winter Barn* even though he had never read it.

Winter Barn through Mark's eyes	
How the crosscutting concepts form the framework for scientific thinking *	
Pattern	The weather shown in the illustrations is consistent with a winter pattern.
Cause and effect	The cold weather causes the animals to move indoors. Hunger causes some animals to eat others.
Structure and function	The structure of the barn serves its function: it shelters the animals.
Scale, proportion, and quantity	The barn is a large environment for the mouse and ants but not for the horse.

Systems and system models	The barn is a system with interacting parts (the animals) within a boundary (walls) and can be viewed as a model for a larger ecosystem.
Energy and matter	Because it is winter, it is getting colder and colder, which means energy (heat) is leaving the system. Animals (matter) seek shelter in this system (the barn).
Stability and change	The barn may be filled with activity but this system is stable because we can predict the daily routine, even when the cat eats the mouse.

*Crosscutting concepts reprinted from Next Generation Science Standards (2013)

Winter Barn, a realistic work of fiction, is not a science book per se, but when you have developed the habits of mind of a scientist, every book has the potential to be a science book. When Valerie says *plot*, Mark thinks *cause and effect*. When a new character enters the story, Mark suspects that change is coming because new energy and matter have been added to the system. Just as a historical and cultural perspective often enriches our experience of a book, when we learn to read like Mark, we add the lens of the scientific world to our understandings.

The Case for This Book

Valerie and her students were intrigued by how Mark interpreted this story through a scientific lens, and during the ensuing discussion, they concluded that they now viewed the book differently. This is not to imply that they had missed anything in their first reading, but rather they had deepened their understanding of this story by adding an additional lens.

The nature of teaching elementary children is that we teach all subjects. True integrative teaching means that each new lens is not additive, but rather it is synergistic. Each of the crosscutting concepts can be seen in all types of literature, and learning to see them enhances the reading experience itself while simultaneously developing the mindset necessary to think like a scientist. This is why we see literature as an authentic context for helping students see science concepts everywhere.

The Challenge of Time

Our school days are packed; districts add to our curriculum yet never suggest what we might omit, and rarely give us extra time. Donald Graves famously described the school day as following the "cha cha cha curriculum" (Harste 2003), observing that teachers and students often sprint through the day from one subject to the next, with little time to delve meaningfully into anything. Decades later, Nell Duke (2016) notes the same concern. "It's not surprising that we feel a press for time. Our expectations for students have increased dramatically, but our actual class time with students has not." In addition to the packed days, because science is rarely on state tests, too often it's thought of as an extra topic that "we'll get to if we have time." The result is that in schools, we may think of science as this thing set apart from other curriculum, something we do on its own, and yet actually, science is everywhere, in everything. In an interview, Sneed B. Collard (2011) captures the integral nature of science perfectly:

> Science is not this thing over here. Science is part of everything we are and everything we do. It affects our economy, it affects our relationships, it affects what we want to eat, it affects who we are attracted to in life. Every aspect of our lives is part of science. And so understanding science, to me, is understanding ourselves.

As we learn to think like scientists, we begin to see science everywhere. On her daily walks, Valerie understands the construction projects better as she now ponders scale and energy as well as structure and function. When she flips through a picture book, scale and pattern jump out of the illustrations. She is finding that this mindset also informs her thinking about personal issues. When a colleague confided to Valerie that she was losing a friendship, Valerie's new lens compelled her to view this as an example of stability and change—although she refrained from comforting her colleague in these terms.

The challenge of time is not going away, but by simply deepening your understanding of the crosscutting concepts, you will begin to see how to infuse your day with talking and thinking about science. And although we certainly hope students will still have many opportunities to actually engage with science in classrooms, *thinking* scientifically doesn't have to be something they turn on and off with a schedule.

A Mindset for Making the Strange Familiar

Culturally, many of us have science heebie-jeebies because the language isn't familiar and the volume of content knowledge is daunting. It isn't that scientists are smarter than everyone else; it is just that the framework based on the crosscutting concepts helps them organize, see, and talk about scientific ideas more easily. Remember, this is why our goat researcher and meteorologist can talk to each other and both can engage a geologist. Regardless of their discipline, they share a conceptual framework built around pattern, causes, systems, and energy, to name a few.

Many of us learned science by memorizing content and then we tried to understand how these lists of facts fit into some larger framework. Scientists approach content differently; they view content through the mindset formed by the crosscutting concepts. When a scientist sees a sharply curved bird beak, because she understands structure and function, she already knows this is a raptor who feeds on flesh. We all want our students to develop an understanding of how things work, and the secret is not memorizing content but rather understanding the concepts. Once the crosscutting concepts are part of our thinking, the content comes more easily because it follows a familiar pattern. For example, all scientists already know that if something is happening, there is a cause and energy is involved. Because the concepts shape their thinking, they already know to ask, "What is the energy that is fueling that effect?" This is what it means to think like a scientist: to use the crosscutting concepts as a schema for conceptualizing, organizing, and understanding our world.

Children's Literature and Science: A Surprisingly Powerful Friendship

Science is a tangible, germane, and integral part of life and, fortunately, is pervasive in children's literature. Because classrooms are filled with books, students have seemingly endless opportunities to build scientific understandings through reading. This book will help you and your students develop the mindset for seeing science as you read, and it will introduce you to the vocabulary for talking about what you see. All books offer possibilities for talk about the crosscutting concepts in the illustrations and text once you know how to look for them.

Our experience with *Winter Barn* helped us see that children's literature is a natural avenue for learning science, and it was a small step to realize that read-alouds could be leveraged to enhance the science curriculum. As we said earlier—and it bears repeating—the ideas we set out in this book are not meant to replace science class; rather, they will show you how children's books can be a powerful ally for moving science beyond a forty-five-minute period and for developing the mindset that will help your students think, talk, and read like scientists all of the time. Soon they will start to see structure and function in a basketball hoop on the playground and in an illustration of a moat in a book about castles.

Seeing the Science in Illustrations

Illustrations invite us to notice what's happening and name the concepts that present themselves visually. When we apply our scientific mindset to an illustration showing a cat frantically scrambling up a tree, we know that there is a cause, there is energy involved, and the structure of the cat's claws are what enables it to climb. We may even deduce that this is a pattern and the mechanism is the neighbor's dog. Once we develop the habit of mind of seeing the crosscutting concepts, we notice them in literally every illustration.

Hearing the Science in Language

Just as the crosscutting concepts are in every illustration, our language is steeped in these same ideas. Sometimes the conceptual language is really obvious, as it is in a nonfiction science book that explains how wind turbines work. We expect to see these books filled with science vocabulary because their purpose is to help us learn about these topics. The science language in fiction, poetry, and other nonscience genres is more subtle, but if you have the ears to hear it, you'll find opportunities to learn and talk about these concepts with this literature as well.

One big and delightful surprise in writing this book was discovering how our daily language reflects the concepts in direct and subtle ways. When we hear *because* we are referring to a cause-and-effect relationship. Many of us use Goldilocks' scale when we want to convey that something is "just right." "I am spinning my wheels" is another way of saying "I am wasting energy." Clearly, Sneed Collard's observation that our lives are filled with science holds true for language as well. To think like a scientist is to see the crosscutting concepts in our language every time we listen, speak, read, or write. As we all know, the trick to learning any new language, including science language, is to use it daily in meaningful contexts. As you read to your students, you will have plenty of opportunities to help the crosscutting concepts become second nature.

What You Will Find in This Book

We have organized the book by dedicating a chapter to each of the seven crosscutting concepts. Chapters 2, 3, and 4 (pattern, cause and effect, and structure and function) are the foundational concepts for thinking like a scientist and for this reason we suggest starting with these. The remaining four concepts (scale, systems and system models, energy and matter, and stability and change) build on the first three and are related because they address the nature of a system. Because the concepts build on each other, they will make the most sense if you approach them in order.

A Primer on the Concept

Each chapter follows a pattern: In the first half we offer a primer titled *Learning and Teaching the Science*, basically everything you need to know to bring this concept into your classroom. If you are the type of person who rushes right to the "quick start" when you buy a new device or appliance, you'll feel right at home with our quick start, which presents a condensed definition and go-to questions that will get you to the heart of each concept. The primer is more than just the content that defines the concept, so we also provide strategies to help you spot the concept and ways to prompt your students to see it. Even if you are completely unfamiliar with the concept, by the end of the primer, you will have the tools and confidence to explore the idea with your students.

Connecting the Concept to Children's Literature

You're probably already reading excellent books to your students, and these same books are exactly what you'll need to begin discussing the crosscutting concepts. The rich illustrations and descriptive narrative that make any book worth having in your classroom library will also support your science discussions. To help you get started, we provide a list of suggested titles in each chapter (many of which you probably already have). You might also consult lists of award winners, like the Orbis Pictus Award (National Council of Teachers of English) for non-fiction and the Caldecott for illustration. One of our go-to resources is the National Science Teachers Association's webpage that highlights outstanding science trade books: www.nsta.org /publications/ostb/. You will notice that there are authors and illustrators who reliably make topics like animal mouths and Queen Victoria's bathing machine fascinating reads. Some of our current favorite nonfiction authors include Sandra Markle, April Pulley Sayre, Gail Gibbons, Steve Jenkins, Patricia Hubbell, Melissa Stewart, and Sneed B. Collard III.

Like all readers, we love to be pulled into the spell that authors and illustrators work so hard to weave when they write books. We want to step out of the way the first time a reader hears Amy Ludwig VanDerwater's poetry or a new book by Steve Jenkins. But we hope to convince you that these books can serve double duty and that by returning to them, you can help your students develop the mindset of thinking like a scientist.

Books That Shout the Concept

Picture books present opportunities to explore the crosscutting concepts through their illustrations and complementary text. In our explorations, we have noticed that some books *shout* about these concepts but others *whisper*. You will find that just about every book you already have in your classroom either shouts or whispers about a crosscutting concept. What does this mean? Shout books are specifically about the concept and call attention to the idea through both text and illustration—it's the focus of the book. For example, *Bridges Are to Cross* (Sturges) and *What Do You Do with a Tail Like This?* (Jenkins) both shout structure and function. Each chapter offers tips on how to identify shout books confidently. Just as it's easier to learn to ride a bike with training wheels, choosing books that are specifically about one of the concepts will help your students develop a framework for thinking about and noticing this concept in all books.

The "topic spotlight" section in each chapter will help you connect the concepts to familiar topics. For example, water, bridges, and seasons are a natural way to approach cause and effect, structure and function, and pattern, respectively. Our goal in this section is to show how you might apply the crosscutting concept to a common science curriculum topic.

Books That Whisper the Concept

Once you develop the tools for identifying a concept where it's obvious, you begin to see it everywhere and even make connections to the concept beyond the discipline of science. When this happens, you will see that most books whisper about different concepts; they give you clues that invite you to explore the concepts during read-aloud or discussion. For example, unlike a book specifically about bridges, the folktale "The Three Billy Goats Gruff" is not about structure and function; nevertheless, the troll's bridge whispers a chance to talk about this concept. Talking about the crosscutting concepts in whisper books allows students to apply their growing understandings to lots of different contexts. Practice first with books that shout the concept (remember these are your intellectual training wheels), and then take any book for a spin to try out your new science lens.

Callie saw that over the course of the year, her students learned to naturally read and think like scientists as a result of rich conversations like the one about Charlotte's web. For example, after revisiting the beloved *Where the Wild Things Are* (Sendak) with her class, she asked how long Max's visit to his fantasy world was. After a brief pause, Kalissa said, "Not long because his dinner was still hot." Kalissa used her understanding of energy and energy transfer to deduce that not much time had passed. This is what it is means to read and think like a scientist. When you see this happening, you will know that your students are wearing their science lens with confidence and that their reading and growing scientific understandings are working synergistically to deepen their understanding of the world.

References

Benedict, Susan, and Lenore Carlisle. 1992. *Beyond Words: Picture Books for Older Readers and Writers*. Portsmouth, NH: Heinemann.

Collard, Sneed B. 2011. *Reading Rockets* interview. April 26. https://www.youtube.com /watch?v=Xv44vuQdi1M&feature=related.

Duke, Nell K. 2016. "What Doesn't Work: Literacy Practices We Should Abandon." *Edutopia*, June 3. www.edutopia.org/blog/literacy-practices-we-should-abandon-nell-k-duke.

Harste, Jerome. 2003. What Do We Mean by Literacy Now?" *Voices from the Middle* 10 (13): 8–12.

Next Generation Lead States. 2013. *Next Generation Science Standards: For States, by States*. Washington, DC: The National Academies Press.

2

PATTERN

Learning and Teaching the Science

What You Need to Know: *Patterns Are Repeats That Have a Cause*

Last summer, third grader Zander was catching small fish on the beach when he came across a juvenile stingray in the shallows feeding on sand fleas (a type of crustacean). Later, he commented that he had never seen a fish quite like the stingray. When asked how he knew it was a fish, he said, "It looked like a fish, swam, and had gills." When asked if the sand flea was a fish, Zander said, "No, it looked like a bug that lives in the water." Zander observed a pattern—the stingrays looked and behaved like fish but the sand fleas did not—and was able to deduce that stingrays are fish and sand fleas are not. As we will explore in this chapter, recognizing and using pattern is the foundation for thinking like a scientist (Figures 2.1 and 2.2).

A pattern is defined as anything that repeats when there is a cause for that repetition. When we asked a class of third and fourth graders to define pattern, they quickly gave the

Figure 2.1
How do you know a house when you see one? It fits a recognizable pattern like Olivia's drawing.

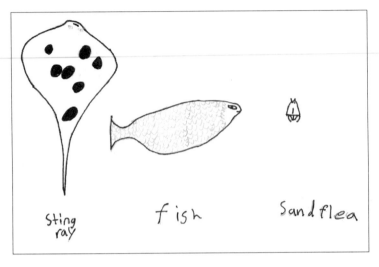

Figure 2.2
Zander knows a stingray is a fish.

example of counting by threes and the alternating colors drawn in Ali's notebook. These are great examples of pattern, but in science *pattern* is also used more broadly to describe relationships, defining characteristics of objects and organisms, as well as physical and biological outcomes, and even behaviors. What all of these patterns have in common is that they are predictable outcomes caused by the principles and laws of the natural world. For example, we all know an oak leaf when we see one because we're familiar with the consistent features of oak leaves: their shape is caused by an inheritance pattern. The sun sets and rises in a predictable pattern because of the way the earth rotates and orbits the sun. Because he recognized a pattern in the kinds of features fish have, Zander knew the stingray was a fish. In the engineered world, patterns are caused by human intent, like a checkerboard or the trusses on a bridge.

That's a pattern? Yes, because something repeats and it has a cause.

Type of Pattern	Example	Repetitive Element	Cause
Mathematical	• Counting by threes • Alternating stripes in Zeb's drawing	• Increases by units of three • Red/blue/red/blue alternating color	• Natural world: mathematical principle • Human intent: aesthetic choice
Biological outcome	• Blue-eyed parents give birth to blue-eyed children	• Eye color	• Natural world: genetics principle

Type of Pattern	Example	Repetitive Element	Cause
Physical outcome	• Muffins rising	• Baking soda leavens	• Natural world: chemical reaction
Organism	• Bird	• Defining characteristics such as beaks, feathers, wings	• Natural world: evolution
Object	• Rubik's Cube	• Defining characteristics: equal sides, six colors	• Human intent and mathematical principle
Behavior	• Geese migrate for winter • Response to receiving a gift	• Canada geese fly south every fall • "Thank you"	• Natural world: evolution • Human intent: socialization

Even though patterns are repetitious, they are not always exact; many are imprecise and you can even see this in your classroom. Take the color brown, for instance. All of your students with brown eyes might be defined as "brown-eyed," but we're willing to bet they have different hues of brown. We all know the color brown when we see it because it fits the pattern we know as brown even if that brown is taupe, chestnut, or chocolate. Imprecise patterns, like different shades of the same color, are still repetitious and recognizable. Some patterns even have a random element embedded within the pattern. Tornado alley in the Midwest was given this name because the right weather conditions form there during certain times of the year, creating a pattern. However, exactly when and where the tornadoes strike is random within the alley.

As Neil deGrasse Tyson points out, people are hard-wired to see pattern. He explains the success of humans as a species in the documentary *Cosmos*: "The best thing we had going for us is our intelligence, especially our gift for pattern recognition." We see this intuitive trait every day in our classrooms. In the block corner, children use pattern recognition to find the same-size blocks to build a wall. They recognize the defining patterns of the different Legos, sorting by size and color to create their own patterns. Students come to school with patterns already embedded in their lives; like all of us, they navigate life by using patterns. Along the way we all learn what a typical or expected pattern is, what patterns are healthy (think diet, sleep, and street safety), and what patterns can be dangerous (poisons, disease, and fire).

Recognizing patterns is as integral to science as salt is to cooking. We once heard a chef say that salt is the superhero of cooking, and we are convinced that pattern is the superhero of science. It is in just about everything. Cause-and-effect relationships are patterns, patterns emerge through evolution, and genetics is the study of inherited patterns. We often base our hypotheses on suspected patterns, and our experiments test if the pattern is real or a random event. Statistics is the mathematical tool we use to validate a suspected pattern. When scientists measure frequency, change, or rates, they are looking for patterns. Patterns can be described and conceptualized using models and theories. Scientists require large sample sizes to reveal hidden or subtle patterns. In short, there would be no science without patterns.

Developing Your Lens: A Key Idea and Three Superpowers

Early in the school year, students learn how to use the room, how the day unfolds, which days their class has art, music, or library, and these become recognizable patterns. Your students would undoubtedly be able to identify these patterns a few weeks into the school year if you asked them. How do they know? There is something repetitious about it. You might ask, "Which day do you need to bring your library books?" "Who knows what we will do after recess tomorrow?" "Who gets dismissed first, the walkers or bus riders?" The goal of questions like these is to have students internalize the key idea: *patterns are repeats.* To help your students see that *patterns have a cause,* you might then ask, "Why do you bring your library books on Tuesdays?" So you can exchange them for a new read. "Why do the walkers get dismissed before the bus riders?" So they can use the crosswalks before the buses are moving.

Clean Your Room, I Can't Find Anything!

What is it about a disheveled room that bothers us? Does it push your buttons when you walk into a messy room? You have probably said, "I can't find anything in here." Being natural pattern seekers, when the pattern is disrupted as it is in a messy room, it takes more mental thought to navigate the space, and it really is harder to find things because pattern is how we locate objects. We expect to find the blocks in the block corner and not under Hawa's desk because that's the pattern. When we tell our children, "It's time to pick-up," we're really saying, "Time to re-establish the pattern."

Patterns Are Repeats
Patterns Are Repeats
Patterns Are Repeats

This is the take-home message for pattern—if there is a pattern, then there is some sort of repetitive element. The repeat, or repetitive element, can be just about anything, but we find that most of the patterns we encounter in classrooms fit into four categories (you might even call this a pattern), and there are different ways to ask, "What repeats?" depending upon the type of pattern.

Physical Characteristics of Objects and Organisms. This is a broad category that includes color (skunks are black and white), shape (floor tiles may be square), texture (sandpaper is rough), parts of an organism (horses have tails), and size (hobbits are small) to name a few. When we see students grouping or sorting objects such as Legos, buttons, cards, or pinecones, we might ask them, "How do you know this is a Lego and not a button? What's the Lego pattern?" The defining characteristics of the colors, bumps, and shapes indicate that this object should go with the other Legos instead of in the button pile. Seven-year-old Ike used a defining characteristic to identify his rock: "Do you want to know how I know it's a geode? It has shiny bumps inside of it." The key to remember is that we recognize things because we are familiar with the pattern that defines them. This is why we know a duck when we see one and do not mistake it for an eagle.

Physical and Biological Outcomes. The natural world is filled with patterns such as chemical reactions and genetic inheritance. We see physical outcomes in action every time we bake our favorite brownies. We know this recipe will repeatedly produce the sweet and tasty morsels we crave (if we do it right) because chemical reactions are also a predictable pattern (e.g., baking soda leavens). We take for granted many of the patterns we observe in biology, which is why we never wonder whether our pregnant cat will give birth to wombats and not kittens. Use the phrase *What happened?* or *What will happen?* to help your students see these types of patterns. Remind them that they can predict the outcome because it is a pattern.

Behavior. Behavior deserves its own category because the way humans and animals respond to any situation very often reflects a predictable pattern. Because we have been socialized, we know when to applaud and when to listen in the auditorium. When someone says, "Thank you," we typically respond with "You're welcome." To "misbehave" such as writing *Patterns are repeats* three times as a heading in a book is to disrupt the accepted pattern for a situation.

Animals also follow behavioral patterns based on evolution, for example when bees swarm or geese fly south for the winter. To help your students see a behavioral pattern ask, "What do you expect they will do?"

Mathematics and Cycles. Some patterns are best described mathematically and these permeate the elementary math curriculum. Counting by fives reveals a pattern whether you start at three or zero. Multiplication arrays are visual patterns created by the repeats of a specific number. Cycles are also math-based patterns. Every seven days a new week begins and it takes roughly 365 days for the earth to orbit the sun. Cycles are sequences that repeat over time such as seasons, sunsets, moon phases, and the development of organisms (caterpillars change into butterflies). The key to identifying cycles is recognizing that the same sequence of events repeats whether it be the phases of the moon, the days of the week, or the life cycle of your favorite butterfly. When asked if the butterfly lifecycle is a pattern, five-year-old Henry replied, "Yeah, it just goes round and round, the butterfly circle." You can help your students see mathematical and cyclical patterns by articulating the sequence, "First, this happens and then that happens," followed by, "What comes next? Does this sequence repeat?" Try looking at a calendar to see this at work with weekdays and weekends. Ask students to name the days that they are in school and the days they are not. (See Figure 2.3.)

Figure 2.3
Timmie knows a bird when she sees one; she has identified the bird pattern.

To identify the repeats or repetitive element(s) that make up the pattern, use appropriate questions:

- Objects and organisms: How do I know one (tree, jacket, pie) when I see one? What are the defining characteristics?

- Relationships such as physical and biological outcomes: What will happen or what happened?

- Mathematical or cyclical pattern: What comes next? Does the sequence repeat?

- Behavior: What do you expect they will do?

The Three Superpowers of Pattern: Classifying, Predicting, and Questioning

Once your students realize that patterns are all around them, your next challenge is to help them recognize how pattern is the superhero of science concepts. If you can see the pattern and name the repetitive element, you have evidence that allows you to tap into the power of pattern. If pattern is a superhero, then its superpowers are classifying, predicting, and questioning.

Classifying. At first pass classifying does not seem like a superpower. Really, who cares if we know that an animal is a mammal or marsupial? Why does it matter? The power of classifying is the knowledge you gain when you correctly identify and categorize something. When a medical provider is making a diagnosis, she is trying to determine if your symptoms are consistent with the defining characteristics of an established pattern. You've experienced this if you have ever had your throat swabbed for strep. By classifying the pathogen, the medical provider now knows the appropriate treatment. Similarly, as soon as Zander recognized that the stingray was a fish, he knew quite a bit about it. Zander used the superpower of classification to confirm that the stingray was a fish. Of course, this only works if you are familiar with the defining characteristics of a specific pattern. Classifying is a shortcut for tapping into and then applying prior knowledge. When your school librarian rushes in to share the latest Caldecott winner, you know you will read it to your class right away because your familiarity with this classification tells you that it is a stellar picture book.

Predicting. Because patterns consist of repetitive sequences, outcomes, or defining characteristics, once we recognize them, they allow us to predict future outcomes and understand past events. Even our dogs have figured this out as evidenced by how they greet us each evening at the door expecting a regular treat. Ask your students what they will do tomorrow when the bell rings at recess and they will answer, "Line up to come inside." Scientists also use patterns to understand the past. Ask children what you sang at the last birthday party you attended right before the cake was served. Even though they weren't there, they know the pattern and that you sang "Happy Birthday" (probably off-key). In your staff meeting, you may discuss changes in demographic patterns to predict how many classrooms your school will need in the coming decade.

Patterns are the evidence for prediction, which is one of the reasons pattern is so powerful to science. In the 1850s John Snow, an English physician, observed that people who drank from one water source in London died of cholera but individuals who drank from a different water source did not. He noticed a pattern that he used as evidence to propose changes in how drinking water and sewage should be handled—clearly they should not be mixed. The evidence, derived from patterns, enabled John Snow to predict that the cholera outbreak could be stopped by changing the pattern of well usage. Pattern can be used as evidence and ultimately can influence human behavior.

On the other hand, sometimes what scientists discover is a break in an expected pattern, and these breaks often lead to important new discoveries. For example, when scientists observed that Uranus wasn't moving the way calculations based on gravity *predicted* it should be moving, they hypothesized that there must be another planet out there affecting the orbit of Uranus. This break in the expected pattern eventually led to the discovery of Neptune.

Questioning. Questioning is the superpower that inspires inquiry and gets you to seek the cause (the why) of the effect (the pattern). Asking questions leads to discovery and problem solving in both science and engineering. Observing patterns nudges us to ask why the pattern is the way it is. You may have noticed that hummingbirds are attracted to red flowers. Why? Are they tastier? Do hummingbirds have a favorite color? Or is it something else? These sorts of questions can only be asked because we notice a pattern. Second grader Leah observed that the sprouts she was growing on her classroom windowsill were all leaning in one direction, and this pattern led her to wonder if plants grow toward light. If we had not documented the rise—a change in the pattern—of global temperatures then we wouldn't know to ask if the climate is changing. Asking questions based on patterns leads us to wonder about cause-and-effect relationships, which is the first step to understanding how and why things work.

That's Not a Pattern, It's a Coincidence!

Like all superheroes, pattern has an arch nemesis: coincidence. Just like Lex Luthor tries to foil Superman, coincidence may obscure our ability to see pattern. Earlier we defined pattern as anything that repeats that has a cause. Coincidence disguises itself as pattern by appearing to

QUICK START FOR
Activating the Superpowers

After identifying the pattern, you can activate the three superpowers by using these go-to questions:

- Classifying: How do I know one when I see one and what do I already know about it? If we only said, "It's a mammal," you would immediately know that it has hair, lactates, and, with a few exceptions, gives live birth. Classifying allows you to tap into and apply prior knowledge.

- Predicting: What can I predict? Pattern allows you to make hypotheses based on the evidence provided by the pattern.

- Questioning: What is causing this pattern? Remember the definition of pattern contains cause. The cause is either human intent or from the natural world.

repeat, but in reality it is nothing more than a series of random events because it lacks cause. Imagine that one of your students says to you, "I just flipped this coin six times and got heads-tails-heads-tails-heads-tails! It must be magic." Our experience (think large sample size) tells us that it was a coincidence and that if the student kept flipping the coin, the suspected pattern would dissolve. So, how do you distinguish between a pattern and coincidence? Sample size and cause. A large sample size gives you confidence that the pattern is real and not a coincidence. You can even use mathematics (statistics) to calculate how confident you are. If your student bought the coin at a magic store, you might suspect that the coin is rigged to alternate outcomes (the cause), but you would be more confident in this idea if you flipped the coin one hundred more times and got the heads-tails-heads-tails pattern.

Because pattern recognition is an innate human quality, we sometimes leap to conclusions and call a coincidence a pattern. Take nine-year-old Nell who had begun to pack her own lunch. She mastered the tuna, cucumber, and peanut butter and jelly sandwiches, and that winter, the whole family noticed that whenever she made PB&J, it snowed. Is this a pattern or a coincidence? Unless Nell knows something about meteorology that the rest of us do not, this is a coincidence. There is no cause and if winter was as long as when the white witch ruled Narnia, the suspected pattern would eventually fall apart. In other words, Nell's sandwich does not cause it to snow. There appears to be a correlation—they occur together—but there is no cause. As we explore in Chapter 3, finding the cause of a pattern is the ultimate proof that it is not a coincidence.

Exploring Pattern in Children's Literature

Picture books present opportunities to explore pattern through genre, layout, language, topics, and illustrations. Just as salt is found in almost every recipe, pattern appears in every genre. Stories themselves contain patterns; in fiction, there are major and minor characters that appear throughout the story, we anticipate that plots will take twists and turns, and we expect that there will be a resolution. In folktales and fairy tales, readers often expect that the number three will play a starring role. There are three daughters ("Beauty and the Beast"), three wishes, and three bowls of porridge. Many forms of poetry are shaped by patterns, such as a specified number of syllables, parts of speech, rhyme, and rhythm. Nonfiction often contains a table of contents, captions, labels, diagrams, and a glossary that constitute a predictable layout. Knowing these patterns gives us a head start and is actually what makes us effective readers. Using the super-power of prediction, we anticipate the characteristics or patterns that make each genre familiar to us before we have even read the book.

Take the layout of a picture book: the number of pages is divisible by eight, the illustration medium typically follows a pattern within a book (think how surprised you would be if an illustrator changed from collage to gouache to pastel), and there is a dedication, a copyright, and the kids' favorite, About the Author. We can predict that just about any book we pick up will follow these patterns. Not only does the layout of books follow a pattern, after all that is how we know it is a book and not a sand flea, but the text also follows a pattern. At a very basic level, language is a pattern and we can see this in its structure and grammar; sentences begin with a

Read Like a Superhero

You will recognize that the superpowers are themselves effective reading strategies and students can learn to activate them through the illustrations or text. When you identify the defining characteristics in an illustration, you are tapping into prior knowledge (classifying). When you see Officer Buckle on the cover of *Officer Buckle and Gloria* (Rathman), you already know that the story will involve a safety officer and a dog. If the story follows a typical pattern (the main character will triumph in the end), you might ask your students to predict (predicting) how the story will unfold. If the pattern is an effect or outcome (think squirrels gathering nuts for winter), then you might ask (questioning), "What's causing this pattern?"

capital and end with punctuation. Word choice often follows a pattern; young readers delight in rhyming text (sound patterns) and repetitive phrases where they can chime in. These patterns allow them to participate because they can predict what to say next. Readers are quick to notice patterns in illustrations such as the same wallpaper in the character's bedroom every time that setting appears. In fact, they might even spot patterns in the design of the wallpaper.

Books That Shout Pattern

People see pattern everywhere, and your classroom library is full of both nonfiction and fiction that *shout* pattern. If we can name an object in an illustration, it is because it fits a pattern we already know; we know a bicycle when we see one because it fits the defining characteristics of the *bike* pattern. Just about every picture book has the potential to be used to discuss pattern with children.

Books that shout often highlight one of the four categories of pattern—physical characteristics of objects and organisms, physical and biological outcomes, mathematics and cycles, and behavior—through striking visuals, word usage, or the story. Equally engaging are books that unexpectedly challenge or break a pattern, which is why the flipped ending of *Brown Bear, Brown Bear, What Do You See?* (Martin) is so satisfying to young readers. Many of the books for beginning readers are crafted just this way, ending with a break in the pattern. Breaking a pattern is a literary strategy for illuminating the pattern. This is true in books for older readers as well. We've all said, "I loved the ending; it took me by surprise." The ending

Now That's a Break in a Pattern

Librarians were sitting on the edge of their seats at the 2008 American Library Association's annual conference waiting for the Newbery and Caldecott Medals to be announced. When the 533-page *The Invention of Hugo Cabret* (Selznick) won the Caldecott Award for picture books, the audience went wild. This lengthy book broke the pattern. What matters is that in breaking the pattern, the judges expanded everyone's view of what a picture book is. Breaking patterns can add to our collective knowledge in literature and in science, and can transform a society (safety standards, inclusive schools, and Civil Rights). Unfortunately, changing a pattern can also be bad (war, new diseases, and reduced school budgets).

of *The Hunger Games* (Collins) is powerful because Katniss and Peeta break the pattern of one ultimate winner.

Many nonfiction titles such as survey books, concept books, and field guides explore a general topic, like trees or insects, and are typically organized by subtopics. These books call attention to pattern on every page, through both text and illustration, as they identify the repetitive elements that make up the pattern such as leaves or wings. Gail Gibbons is famous for this type of book; in *Tell Me, Tree*, for example, readers are introduced to characteristic patterns (trees have wood, leaves, bark, and roots). To explore pattern in nonfiction with your class, look for books that invite the discovery of a repeated behavior (bears hibernate) or phenomenon (seasons change), provide opportunities to group or classify (types of animals or man-made structures), or note a change or break in the pattern (dust bowl or climate change).

In teaching reading, we may not call genre structures *pattern*, but they are. Elements repeat, and readers can classify, make predictions, and ask questions. How do you know a poem, fairy tale, or work of historical fiction when you see one? Because genres have patterns. Fables present morals, fairy tales include magic, and historical fiction includes real events or time periods. These are predictable patterns.

Plots often follow patterns. For example, in the book *The Mitten*, about a classic Ukrainian folktale, we can immediately see the repetitive element: on each page, an animal of slightly larger size climbs into a mitten. Using pattern's superpower of prediction, we know that no car will be driving into the mitten, only animals will enter, and we can predict that on the next page there will be a different animal, slightly larger, that joins the others. As the plot reaches its climax, readers begin to wonder just how many animals can fit, or as Mark would ask, "What's the carrying capacity of this mitten?" Like the straw that breaks the camel's back, this story ends by changing the pattern. When a cricket joins the group, the mitten finally breaks. No matter which version of the folktale you read, the plot shouts pattern and pattern's superpowers are what engage the reader.

Book Selection and Beginning Conversations

Read-alouds provide a daily opportunity to help your students develop their pattern-spotting skills. In books with obvious patterns like *Brown Bear, Brown Bear, What Do You See?* or *The Mitten*, you might ask students to predict what is going to happen or appear on the next page partway through the book. Ask them, "How do they know what is going to happen? What's the pattern that clued you in?"

To extend students' thinking about pattern, pick a book that presents topic surveys (all about bears or buildings) or concepts (shapes) in either the engineered or natural world. Books that feature life cycles (butterflies or plants) are also a great place to start. Look for a book that allows you to talk about physical characteristics, physical and biological outcomes, mathematics and cycles, or behavior. *Some Bugs* (DiTerlizzi) classifies insects using illustrations and witty text. Ask questions like, "How do you know it's a bug? What will happen? What will it do?" to identify the repetitive elements. These are powerful prompts to discover a physical characteristic, outcome, or behavior. Keep in mind that some patterns in the engineered world are based solely on aesthetics or human intent, like *paisley* scarves. Many aesthetic patterns have been stripped of their superpowers because the cause may be whimsy or artistic style, but these aesthetic patterns are all around us (just look at how your students are dressed today), and for this reason identifying these types of pattern are a familiar entry point for developing the habit of identifying patterns.

TALK PROMPTS for exploring different types of pattern in shout books

Use a book like this:	Notice this:	Ask a question like this to engage the superpowers:
To explore physical characteristics of an object (aesthetics)	Each page of *My Dad* (Browne) celebrates the narrator's dad, who metaphorically swims like a fish and eats like a horse. The heartfelt descriptions and illustrations showcase Dad on every page in his signature plaid bathrobe and striped pajamas; these fabric motifs are even echoed on his toast.	To classify, ask: • "How do you know Dad when you see him? What are the visual clues?" To predict, ask: • "What can you predict Dad will be wearing on the next page?" To question, ask: • "Why is Dad wearing striped pajamas and a plaid bathrobe?" Because even if they clash, he likes them—it is an aesthetic choice.
To explore physical characteristics of organisms (natural world)	*Tell Me, Tree* is a classic Gibbons compendium of everything about trees from life cycle to types. Gibbons establishes the characteristics of trees such as bark, wood, leaves, and roots. Field guides shout pattern because they help readers identify a specific pattern—how do we know a pine tree when we see one? When Gibbons provides a thumbnail illustration of pine needles, the reader learns that this is a defining pattern of an evergreen.	To classify, ask: • "How do you know a tree when you see one?" • "When looking at a plant, what clues tell you it is a tree?" To predict, ask: • "If we plant a sapling on Arbor Day, what will it look like in twenty years? How do you know? What is the pattern that enabled you to make this prediction?" To question, ask: • "Why do you think trees are made of wood?" Wood is hard, which allows trees to grow tall without falling over.

continues

Use a book like this:	Notice this:	Ask a question like this to engage the superpowers:
To explore patterns of behavior	*The True Story of the 3 Little Pigs* (Scieszka--rhymes with *Fresca*) humorously retells this classic tale from the wolf's perspective. Older readers will enjoy the challenge of identifying which elements of the pattern are still the same, but they will laugh at the ones that are not. The wolf's perspective deviates from the expected pattern, which is what makes the story funny.	To classify, ask: • "We know that wolves are carnivores. Why does this pattern make him the big bad wolf?" To predict, ask: • "What do you think will happen in this book based on your prior knowledge of the story?" To question, ask: • "Why is the wolf making up excuses for blowing down the house?"
To explore a cycle	Eric Carle's classic *The Very Hungry Caterpillar* provides two opportunities to explore cycle; the most obvious is the metamorphic transition to a butterfly, but the preposterous feast progresses through another cycle— the days of the week.	To classify, ask: • "What are the two cycles in this book and how do you know they are cycles? What repeats?" To predict, ask: • "If you made your own butterfly book, what pattern would you include? If this book had a sequel, what would happen?" To question, ask: • "Why is the caterpillar so hungry?"

As we shared earlier, recognizing pattern and organizing our lives by pattern is an innate quality; writers create based on patterns, illustrators reinforce and complement these patterns, and readers rely on them to make sense of the book. Pattern is one of the easiest concepts to explore through reading. In Figure 2.4 we suggest some of our favorite books for finding pattern. As pattern spotting becomes second nature for you and your students, you will begin to see patterns in every book on your shelf.

Topic Spotlight: Seasons

In many ways we pattern our lives around the seasons. The academic calendar, agriculture, sports, clothing, and holidays are all associated with seasons. Third grader Quinn starts planning his Halloween costume in the early fall. The end of summer signals that soccer season is about to begin to Libby. Felix looks forward to swimming outside in the summer. Seasons and the patterns associated with them are an accessible topic for learning about patterns because students are already familiar with them and how seasons shape their lives.

SEASONS

One Fall Day (Bang)

And Then It's Spring (Fogliano)

The Reasons for Seasons (Gibbons)

Awesome Autumn (Goldstone)

And the Good Brown Earth (Henderson)

In November (Rylant)

Chicken Soup with Rice: A Book of Months (Sendak)

Forest Has a Song (VanDerwater)—poetry

WEATHER/CLIMATE

It's Raining! (Gibbons)

Tornadoes! (Gibbons)

Weather Forecasting (Gibbons)

Tornadoes (Simon)

Weather (Simon)

CYCLES

The Tiny Seed (Carle)

I'll See You When the Moon Is Full (Fowler)

Monarch and Milkweed (Frost)

From Seed to Plant (Gibbons)

Monarch Butterfly (Gibbons)

Butterflies in the Garden (Lerner)

Pumpkin Circle (Levenson)

The Moon (Simon)

GENETICS (INHERITED PATTERNS)

Living Color (Jenkins)

My First Day (Jenkins)

Sisters and Brothers (Jenkins and Page)

COLLECTIONS

Max's Words (Banks)

Everybody Needs a Rock (Baylor)

The Right Word: Roget and His Thesaurus (Bryant)

The Matchbox Diary (Fleischman)

The Puddle Pail (Kleven)

Lots and Lots of Coins (Reid)

The Art Collector (Wahl)

SURVEY BOOKS

Some Bugs (DiTerlizzi)

Bees, Snails, and Peacock Tails (Franco)

Swirl by Swirl: Spirals in Nature (Sidman)

BEHAVIOR

The Doorbell Rang (Hutchins)

Blackout! (Rocco)

Madlenka (Sís)

Figure 2.4

A beginning list of books that shout pattern by category

Being from Vermont, we are partial to the maple tree and like to share *A Tree for All Seasons* (Bernard) with students when exploring the effect of seasons on this iconic tree. The clear photographs and direct text guide the reader through the pattern of cyclical changes in both the weather and the tree brought by winter, spring, summer, and fall. When we asked a second-grade class, "How do you know it's fall? Or spring?" we got responses like, "Every year it (the tree) changes over and over again," and "The leaves change from no leaves to some buds to green leaves to red leaves." The students quickly identified that the tree and weather changed with the seasons, and they also noticed that people's interactions with the tree are shaped by the seasons; in the fall, "kids jumped in the leaves," and Ruba recognized the taps used to collect the sap in the spring. Ezra chimed in with "Squirrels hide their food underground so that they have food for the winter." Here's how to apply the superpower questions to this book or any book about the seasons:

- Classifying (tapping into prior knowledge about the topic): Ask, "How do you know what time of year it is? What are the clues? How do you know a maple tree when you see one? A chipmunk? A sugaring tap?"

- Predicting: Ask, "What will the tree look like in spring? Summer?"

- Questioning (What is the cause?): Ask, "Why do the leaves turn red and fall off? Why are the seeds shaped like a helicopter? Why do the leaves come out in the spring?"

Books That Whisper Pattern

Our lives are a series of patterns. As we write, the leaves are starting to change color in Vermont, a pattern that indicates fall is here and winter is on its way. We might even say that pattern is always *whispering* in the background even if we don't label it as pattern. It's easy to forget to name this as a pattern because it is so embedded in our lives, but this is what it means to read and even live like a scientist—to make these whisperings explicit and then engage their superpowers. We find that this is also true of books. Many of them whisper clues about pattern such as the passing of a season as shown by a character's clothing or leaves on a tree changing. These clues invite us to identify the pattern during a read-aloud or discussion.

Language is another powerful way to hear the whispers of pattern. Listen for words that often refer to pattern such as: *next, again, then, last time, repeat, calendar, behavior, schedule, routine, normal, dangerous, group, typical, expected, stable,* or *fashionable*. Some of these may not immediately be recognized as words that describe pattern (and depending on context they might not), but challenge your students to see if they can name how each of these words is pattern related. To see your daily *routine* as a pattern is to recognize that you repeat certain behaviors and activities.

In whisper books, patterns may not be front and center but you can still see them and activate their superpowers using the text and/or illustrations. Identify the repetitive element and then summon the questions. In many ways, whisper books are better for teaching pattern than shout books. You have to work harder to find the pattern, which helps students develop the habit of mind of spotting pattern, even subtle ones. To be a scientist is to be a pattern spotter and literature whispers it everywhere. Consider, for example, how you might approach pattern in a whisper book using *The Day the Crayons Quit* (Daywalt), a humorous picture book where letters from different-color crayons complain about their roles in drawings.

TALK PROMPTS to help you notice pattern in books that whisper

Prompts for spotting pattern in any book	How these would look in a discussion about *The Day the Crayons Quit*
Choose an object in the book, identify it, and then explain the defining characteristics of the pattern that allowed you to identify it. In other words, how do you know a *duck* when you see one? What do you already know about this classification?	Ask students how they know a crayon when they see one. The patterns of crayons are easily identified by the characteristic wrapper and monochromatic pointy and flat end, and they provide color in drawings.
During read-aloud, pause partway through the book and predict what will come next in either the story or the illustrations. (Predicting)	Read a few of the letters. Then predict what other colors might complain about. Each crayon complains about being stereotyped or overworked or being usurped by another color.
If the pattern is in the natural world, what is its cause?	Crayons are in the engineered world so this question does not apply to this book.
If the pattern is in the engineered world, is the cause aesthetic or functional? If it is functional, what's it doing? (Questioning)	The cause of the complaints is aesthetic choice. The crayons are not happy with their culturally assigned roles; red feels it is used in too many firetrucks and is sick of working on holidays.

People love patterns. Fashion is filled with them (think argyle socks), and people collect all sorts of things like buttons, coins, and antique fish lures based on patterns that appeal to them. Sports fans banter about patterns when trying to predict who is going to win on game day, and

Valerie collects tea bag labels to use for collage projects. Clearly pattern recognition is satisfying and even fun, but the power of pattern is so much more than this. Superheroes routinely save the world, and pattern can change our world by altering human behavior for the better. Scientists notice patterns with negative consequences and suggest changes to the patterns, and ideally we change our behavioral patterns for the better. This is what preventive medicine is all about. This is why we now cough in our elbows, wear helmets, and wash our hands before eating and after going to the bathroom. Thanks to John Snow most of us do not have to worry about cholera daily—we know that fecal matter is not in our drinking water. Superheroes save people in miraculous ways but pattern is not miraculous, it is right there in front of us. Our challenge is to recognize patterns, use them as evidence for predictions, and then build and create new technologies, change our patterns of behavior for the better, and ultimately reshape the world around us.

3

CAUSE AND EFFECT

Making Ripples

Learning and Teaching the Science

What You Need to Know: *If Something Happens There Is a Cause*

Your typical four-year-old in the why phase has all of the makings of a stellar scientist. Young children, like scientists, are trying to understand their world, and "What happened?," "Why did it happen?," and "How did it happen?" are the right questions to ask. To be a scientist is to channel your inner four-year-old and apply these questions because they reveal the critical elements of cause-and-effect relationships. Cause and effect form a relationship because you can't have an effect without a cause (and yes, this means that there is no magic). (See Figure 3.1.)

We like to use a playground puddle or a bucket of water to explore these key ideas of cause and effect with students. Think about a time when you watched your students on the playground tossing rocks into a puddle after a rain. Before the rock was tossed, the surface of the water was flat and calm.

Figure 3.1
When Olivia draws smoke coming out of the chimney, we know there is a cause.

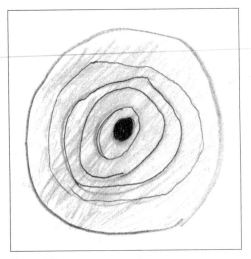

Figure 3.2

Ripples forming in a puddle

What happened after the rock landed in the puddle? The *effect* is that a ripple formed. *Why* did the ripple form? The stone hitting the surface *caused* the ripple. *How* did the ripple form? The stone's volume displaced water, which created ripples. *What, why,* and *how* are the go-to words for discovering the effect (what), the cause (why), and the mechanism (how). (See Figure 3.2.) You can do this same demonstration on the playground or with a bucket of water.

To see cause and effect in action, look around—doesn't matter where you are. Cause and effect happens all around us every day, but the key to thinking like a scientist is to remember that if something happens, there is a cause. The wind blowing outside of your classroom window is causing the tree to sway. The battery in Talia's laptop is causing her computer to work, but the low power icon may cause her to plug it in. A bird takes flight outside and a few seconds later you see the cause: a cat appears from around the corner. All of these are cause-and-effect relationships because you couldn't have the effect if there wasn't a cause.

Look for the mechanism—that's how the cause works. You might think of it as the cause of the cause. In the puddle experiment, the stone caused the ripples because the stone displaced the water—that's the mechanism. Add the word *mechanism* to your vocabulary and you'll be glad you did. Mechanism is what scientists seek to help them understand the natural world. When scientists ask, "What is the mechanism?" they are asking, "How does it happen?" Mechanism is about seeing how the cause-and-effect relationship works. So how do you start to see mechanisms in cause-and-effect relationships? It's about noticing and asking the catchphrase, "If it's happening, how?" That's the mechanism.

For example, when you cook a whole egg, you already know the effect (hard-boiled) and the cause (cooking), but the mechanism is how the heat changes the proteins in the egg. Cause-and-effect relationships are powerful because they entice us to seek the mechanisms, and when we find them, they help us understand the rules that govern the natural and engineered worlds. To get students to think about mechanism, ask them, "Why do ripples form in the puddle?" Because the stone's volume displaced the water. Next ask, "What would happen if we tossed a bigger rock into the puddle?" The ripples caused by the rock would be larger because the larger rock displaces more water. This simple experiment will allow you to introduce a cause-and-effect relationship and allow you to explore the mechanism.

Developing Your Lens: Just Ask, "What, Why, and How?"

What Happened? Why? Spotting a Cause-and-Effect Relationship

The effect is *what happened*; it is what you can see or measure such as a bird flying away, the amount of coffee left in your cup, or rain clouds forming in the afternoon. *Why it happened* is the cause. If your child is sick (the effect), you wonder why—what caused it? Identifying cause and effect is part of your life already; we all already assume that the events around us have causes. When one of your students walks in from recess with a skinned knee, you inevitably ask, "Did you fall?" If you leave the milk out overnight, you sniff it before drinking it, anticipating the sour effect. As you develop the habit of mind of seeing cause and effect, listen for the word *because* (wait for it) because it tells you, "Here comes the cause." We might even say, "The milk is spoiled because it was left out overnight."

How Did It Happen? Understanding Mechanism

The cause tells us *why* something happens, but asking *how* it happens reveals the mechanism. The mechanism is how the cause works. Take a pencil, place it in a sharpener, and turn the handle. The effect is that the pencil is sharp and the cause is you turning the handle. The mechanism is the spiral blades turning clockwise shaving the wood and graphite into a point. We all know that we start a car (effect) by turning the key or pushing a button (cause). The mechanism is how it happens: a circuit is connected, a current flows to the spark plugs, and combustion occurs in the cylinder. When students recover from strep throat (effect) by taking antibiotics (cause), the mechanism is inhibition of bacterial growth by the drug. Just as if there is an effect there is a cause, if there is a cause there is a mechanism, and as we will explain, mechanisms are governed by the principles and laws of chemistry, biology, and physics—what we like to call *the rules*.

Cause-and-effect relationships are governed by these rules; it is in fact the rules that produce the mechanisms. When the wind blows, you can already guess what the leaves will do—they might rustle or get pulled off the tree but they won't change color, sing, or combust—there is no mechanism for these outcomes because the rules don't allow that. As ten-year-old Jax observed, "Wind can't start fires" (although it can spread them).

To think like a scientist is to remember that if it happens in the natural or engineered worlds, we can find a biological, physical, or chemical explanation for it. Seeking mechanism is the bread and butter for scientists and is a great skill to begin to develop in students. Sometimes the mechanism is accessible (the stone displaced the water), and other times you have to know the relevant principles of biology, chemistry, or physics. Look for opportunities to seek mechanism in your science curriculum. None of us know all of these rules, but just remember if it happened, there is a way in which it happened, a mechanism. Because it is not possible to know every mechanism, to read like a scientist is to notice cause and effect and always wonder, what is the mechanism? This is why we celebrate our most skeptical students; they are the mechanism seekers. Once this understanding becomes a part of your scientific lens, the next steps could be to design a way to research the mechanism.

Cause-and-Effect Relationships Are Often Patterns

You might already have noticed that cause-and-effect relationships are often a pattern, although some are a one-time or rare event. How do you tell a pattern from a rare event? When you can identify the repetitive element.

Toss a second pebble into our puddle, and you'll get ripples again; it's a pattern of cause and effect. When cause and effect is a pattern, it has the superpowers of classifying, predicting, and questioning and we can even see them in a puddle. You can predict that ripples will form every time you throw in a pebble. You can ask what would happen if you changed the cause (e.g., the shape, density, or size of the pebble). You can even classify the waves by their characteristics. You already use these superpowers in your daily life as do your students. Third grader Mariana doesn't like the tire swing anymore, because she already knows the effect: "It makes me dizzy." Would you bother to smell test milk that had been on the counter for a week? You already know this pattern and can predict the effect; it's definitely spoiled because of the mechanism (bacteria).

Cause-and-Effect Relationships Can Be Multifaceted

Most things in life aren't simple and this is true of cause-and-effect relationships as well. All of our examples so far have been a single cause with a single effect like when a bird flies away because a cat appears. Many cause-and-effect relationships are multifaceted. There is more than one cause and often we do not know all of them. That's what makes these relationships so intriguing to discuss. There may be several reasons why a student is late to school, storms form if numerous conditions are right (which is why the weather is hard to predict), and there is no single cause for cancer. The multifaceted nature of some cause-and-effect relationships makes them difficult to predict. This is why kids, parents, and teachers love to talk endlessly about the likelihood of a snow day. There are many causes to consider in your prediction: When will the storm start? How much will it snow? Will there be ice? How fast will it melt? This is also what's at play in Monday morning quarterbacking.

Pattern, Mechanism, and Truth in Science

Cause and effect not only helps us understand why and how things happen, but it is through understanding this relationship that we arrive at understanding in science. Do you ever wonder how to tell if something is true? Scientists try to meet two criteria: the ability to tell you *what* is going to happen (predictability or reproducibility) and *how* it is going to happen (mechanism). Predictability comes from recognizing a pattern. If you know the pattern, you can predict with certain accuracy. But pattern is often not enough. Take the rooster Chanticleer from Chaucer's *Canterbury Tales* who observed an interesting behavioral pattern: every morning he crows and then the sun rises. In his mind, his crowing causes the sun to rise but we all know he is wrong. There is no rooster that causes the sun to rise because there is no mechanism for this to happen. Predictability without mechanism is simply a correlation. A correlation may be a pattern or it may be a coincidence (remember Nell's sandwich does not cause it to snow). If we take a more serious statement, "Smoking increases the risk of lung cancer," how do we know it is true? For years people had noticed a correlation between smoking and lung cancer but the statement was not shown to be true until the mechanism was discovered—cigarette smoke contains carcinogens. To think like a scientist is to seek mechanism and be a skeptic until you get it. Your watchword should always be *if that's the cause, what's the mechanism?*

QUICK START FOR
Developing Habits of Mind About Cause and Effect

Ask: "What happened?" That's the effect. It is something you can see or measure.

Ask: "Why did it happen?" Because _____. *Because* is the signal word that we use linguistically to convey a cause. Whenever we use this word, we are explaining the reason for the effect. Remember, if there is an effect (something happened), then there is always a cause; it's a relationship.

Ask: "How did it happen?" That's the mechanism. What rules of the natural or the engineered worlds are at play here?

Examples of cause, effect, and mechanism in the natural and engineered worlds

What happened? The effect	Why did it happen? The cause (It happened *because* ...)	How did it happen? The mechanism
Dog wags tail	*because* ... its owner arrives home.	Behavioral response
Toast burns	*because* ... it was left in the oven.	The high temperature burned the flour. The toast was oxidized by the high temperature.
Road erodes	*because* ... there was a flash flood.	High volume and speed of water washed away the sandy soil.
Race bike goes faster	*because* ... it is lighter and aerodynamic.	The bike takes less energy to move it at the same speed.

Exploring Cause and Effect in Children's Literature

In essence, the act of reading is a cause-and-effect relationship, although we may not all experience it in the same way. Reading evokes responses. Louise Rosenblatt's theory of reading as a transaction between the text and the reader explains why some people may cry at the end of a book but others remain stoic. Each reaction (the effect) may be rooted in a reader's personal history or preference (the causes) for one type of book or another. The mechanism in this case might be how our specific life experiences or personality traits shape our responses. As you explore cause and effect with your students, you might ask them to reflect on how they respond to a read-aloud or independent reading and then compare their reactions. What caused them to laugh? What scared or outraged them? What might be the cause of these varied responses (effects)? We joke that after reading *The Hunger Games*, Valerie's reaction was to protest war and Mark's was to build his own arena.

Books That Shout Cause and Effect

In essence, all books shout cause and effect because something *happens* in every book. This particular concept is the clearest, most obvious one to layer into your conversations around read-aloud (so much so that you won't even find a section on books that whisper in this chapter). To explore cause and effect, when you share a book with children, simply talk about what's happening in the book and *why* it's happening to explore this concept. All books shout cause and effect, but the key is to understand that they shout differently in fiction and nonfiction.

First, consider fiction. It's easy to see cause-and-effect relationships in the plotline of fiction and in the relationships between characters, characters and their environment, and even between elements of the environment (wind blows down tree). Stories often end with the resolution (the effect) of the conflict (the cause). What keeps us reading is wondering which effect will be revealed in the end and how the characters get there. How this unfolds *is* the story; the twists and turns of the plot are the mechanisms that keep us reading. Consider *Charlotte's Web* (White). From the outset, we want to know whether the pig will live or die. Will Wilbur end his days at the butcher or in retired contentment with his slops on Zuckerman's farm? Charlotte's efforts save the pig and the mechanism is her uncanny weaving of words like *some pig, terrific,* and *humble* into her web. Books like this, even though they violate the rules of science, can still help your students develop the habit of mind of spotting the cause, effect, and even mechanism.

Fiction writers craft the causes and effects of their stories as a fundamental literary device, and good writers keep us guessing and wanting to know the final effect. Isn't this why we occasionally binge watch a TV season or burn through a book series? Not knowing the resolution piques our interest and keeps us reading until we know what happens (the effect that ends the story). Astute readers quickly identify the role of cliffhangers at the end of chapters, or as third grader Addie explains, "You don't get the answer to what happened." Other accomplished writers end with an uncomfortable effect to invite us to examine cause closely. In Jacqueline Woodson's powerful book, *Each Kindness,* the book ends with the main character, Chloe, expressing sincere regret over how she treated a classmate who moved away. The reader, like Chloe, is unsettled by the ending, and wishes for Chloe to have the chance to go back and make amends by changing the causes of her remorse. What makes this story so powerful is that we are forced to sit with a cause-and-effect relationship that saddens us.

Works of nonfiction, including all-about books, history, and biography, are actually explanations of cause-and-effect relationships. *What Happens to a Hamburger?* (Showers) deftly guides the reader through the digestive process. After reading this book, seven-year-old Juan distilled the cause-and-effect relationship down to its essence: "Digestion, the little bugs eat it up before you poop it out." The chart below considers how cause and effect shouts differently in different genres.

Book Selection and Beginning Conversations

Cause and effect is how writers create, disrupt, and resolve tension in fiction, and for this reason you can choose just about any story to begin a discussion of cause and effect. John Rocco's brilliant book, *Blackout,* is a great example. The story begins with "It started out as a normal summer night" and the youngest child is frustrated in his attempts to persuade family members

Genre	Look for this type of cause-and-effect relationship and mechanism when appropriate	Examples of books
Fiction subgenres		
Traditional literature: just-so stories, pourquoi tales, myths, legends	These books are cultural attempts to explain the causes of natural phenomena.	• "How the Elephant Got Its Trunk" (Kipling) • *Why Mosquitoes Buzz in People's Ears: A West African Tale* (Aardema)
Mystery	Mysteries are typically about trying to discover the cause; after all, that's the whodunit.	• History Mystery series (Yolen and Stemple) • Any of the art mystery novels by Blue Balliett • Kate and Sarah Klise mysteries
History and historical fiction	History explores the causes of historical events (effects). As we all know, this genre offers rich opportunities to explore multifaceted causes for the same event (e.g., World War II on different continents).	• *Bat 6* (Wolff) • *Number the Stars* (Lowry) • *Baseball Saved Us* (Mochizuki)
Contemporary realistic fiction	This genre explores the causes and effects of everyday life such as adjusting to a new home or a new sibling, making friends, or homelessness.	• *Alexander and the Terrible, Horrible, No Good, Very Bad Day* (Viorst) • *I Know Here* (Croza) • *Knuffle Bunny* (Willems) • *The Lady in the Box* (McGovern)
Nonfiction subgenres		
Biography	The effect in this case is the events that define this individual's life and the narrative explores the causes.	• *The Right Word: Roget and His Thesaurus* (Bryant) • *The Noisy Paint Box: The Colors and Sounds of Kandinsky's Abstract Art* (Rosenstock) • *Wilma Unlimited* (Krull)
Nonfiction survey books	Many of these books are about how the principles and laws of the natural world (i.e., *the rules*) cause effects, such as how rotting fruit becomes compost.	• *What Happens to a Hamburger* (Showers) • *Compost Stew* (Siddals)

to play with him. When the power goes out (the cause), family members are forced to abandon their electronic devices and instead enjoy time together on the roof and in the street (the effect). Recognizing and naming the cause-and-effect relationship in picture books like this can begin your class conversation about this concept. When in doubt, asking "What happened?" and "Why did it happen?" followed by "How did it happen?" will get you started.

Cause and effect is everywhere in literature, and to get your students talking about these relationships, be guided by the word *because*. *Because* points us to the cause of an effect: I am late *because*, I am tired *because*, or I am happy *because*. We might recognize that Yukio is exhausted because he woke up before dawn on his birthday. After we identify the cause and effect, it's an easy step here to ask about mechanism: How did waking up before dawn cause Yukio to be exhausted? Because getting up early disrupted his sleep cycle. Once you and your students notice the power of the word *because*, you will see cause-and-effect relationships in every book and hear it in every conversation. Let's consider how to use *because* to reveal a central cause-and-effect relationship in fiction and nonfiction books.

Farmer Duck (Waddell) tells the story of an overworked duck driven to exhaustion (effect) by a lazy farmer (cause). The lazy farmer is shown lolling about in bed, eating bonbons, and asking a tired and bedraggled duck, "How goes the work?" Many illustrations and text show the duck toiling. These images and words tell us that this story is about a multifaceted cause-and-effect relationship between the farmer and the duck. You might craft a statement for your students to complete like "The duck is exhausted because. . . ." Notice how the word *because* connects the cause to the effect. Picture books are filled with many lovely details like the ones that make this book charming, such as the duck wearing an apron while washing dishes or standing on a stool to iron. These types of effects enrich our reading experience but are not directly related to the central cause-and-effect relationship. Saying something like, "The duck is wearing the apron because" will tell you how he keeps his feathers dry, but will not help you understand the cause-and-effect relationship that is the plot. The book ends with the animals ousting the farmer (an effect) because of how he has treated the duck.

You can use the word *because* the same way with nonfiction. *A River Ran Wild* (Cherry) presents the history of how the Nashua River was changed (the effect) by human activity (the cause). Just as with any book, keep in mind that the goal is to identify the text and images that illustrate the central cause-and-effect relationship. Cherry shows early populations coexisting with a clean river because they did not pollute; they hunted and fished for sustenance. In the industrial era, the river is presented as alarmingly orange because of the dye being dumped into it. Images are supported by descriptions such as "Every day for many decades pulp was dumped into the Nashua" that clearly link the cause (industrialization) to the effect (pollution). Here's a great opportunity to begin to think about mechanism. If the cause is

CAUSE

The paper plant was dumping.

EFFECT

The paper plant polluted the river so it turned RED

They put pulp and dye in the river

Mechanism

Figure 3.3

Henry's river drawing

"industrialization," what's the mechanism? The dye is a toxin that kills life. More advanced students could further explore the chemical mechanism by unpacking the word *toxin.* Henry's illustration (Figure 3.3) shows that he understands the cause, effect, and mechanism in this book. Your students already identify cause-and-effect relationships every time they use the word *because,* but helping them articulate the role of this word will help them develop the habit of mind that enables them to read like a scientist.

In addition to *because,* other words also cue cause-and-effect relationships. Verbs ending in *-ing* are always either a cause or an effect depending upon the context. *Running* causes us to be tired, fit, or fast (all effects). We could say, "I am running because the lion is chasing me." In this case running is the effect and the lion chasing is the cause. Words such as *result, conclusion, ending, product, tragedy, crash, consequence, verdict, solution, score, grade, win, loss,* or *laugh* (or any other emotional state) also suggest effect.

We often feel like we are drowning in the great number of cause-and-effect relationships authors use to create rich and nuanced stories through plots, subplots, and character development. How do we decide which we should talk about? Although many relationships are worth exploring, it's best to choose one of the cause-and-effect relationships in the illustrations or the text that matter most to the story. After all, *because* is a powerful word for seeking the cause, but not every cause in a book is worth exploring. If you see a red ball, you could prompt your class with "The ball is red because," but unless you are studying light and color, this cause is probably not germane to your discussion.

To give you an example, we randomly picked an illustration out of *The True Story of the 3 Little Pigs* (Scieszka). On this page, we saw clouds, the sun, grass, stumps, a saw on the ground, and in the center of the page, a log house. In this tale, the pigs build their own houses and so we know to pay attention to the saw, stumps, and log house. The additional effects such as the weather hint at other cause-and-effect relationships not directly related to the story. Looking at cause and effect in the ill-fated second pig's situation, we see the cause and mechanism

TALK PROMPTS for exploring cause and effect in any book

Notice the effect by asking, "What happened?"	To reveal the cause, ask, "Why did it happen?" Use *because* to see if the relationship works as shown below.
In *Blackout* (Rocco), the youngest child is delighted when his family spends a great evening together on the roof of their apartment building and out on their city street.	Because the electricity outage deprived the parents and sister of power for their electronic evening activities, the family reconnects through other pastimes.
A subway station becomes a communal shelter for city residents as they escape a summer thunderstorm in *Tap Tap Boom Boom* (Bluemle).	Because the strong winds, lightning, thunder, and rain force them to seek shelter.
In the true story of *The Boy Who Harnessed the Wind* (Kamkwamba and Mealer), William builds a windmill (the effect) out of scrap materials to generate electricity to bring water to his parched village in Malawi.	There are many causes of this effect: Because electricity is needed to run windmills to pump water, because drought destroyed the maize, because there was no food, and because people began to starve.

represented by the saw and logs, and the effect in the resulting log house. The message from the central cause-and-effect relationship in this story is clear: build with brick.

Topic Spotlight: Eating and Water

Everybody eats and has a complex relationship with water. For these reasons, eating and water are two natural topics for approaching cause and effect. At mealtime children are often reminded of one of the most important cause-and-effect relationships in their lives: you need to eat to have energy and to grow. In a book like *Time to Eat* (Jenkins and Page), each page presents an animal and the particulars of their eating habits. On one page we learn that a tick "may wait years for a meal" but when it finally eats, it consumes the equivalent of 6,000 chocolate milkshakes. To help your students see cause-and-effect relationships on a page like this, ask, "What happens?" and you might get an answer like, "The tick eats a lot, as much as me drinking 6,000 shakes." This is the effect and clearly when ticks eat they really go for it. After the effect has been identified, probe for the cause by asking, "Why does this happen?" and listen for, "Ticks rarely eat." You might want your students to then put these two ideas into a sentence using *because*. "Ticks eat a lot because they rarely eat." When we challenged a second grader to find the mechanism, Thora nailed it, "It's hard for ticks to attach to an animal; they (animals) go too fast."

How do they do that? The key question

In realms where pigs can build houses and characters can turn into owls, fly, or play Quidditch, authors create their own rules. In the world we physically inhabit, if something happens, it is because the rules of biology, chemistry, and physics caused it to happen. This is a powerful realization because it means that all effects can teach us something about the rules (i.e., the mechanisms). To read like a scientist is to ask, "What can I learn about the rules that govern the natural and engineered worlds from these illustrations and text?" A rainbow, magical as it seems, follows the rules of physics, which means that you can understand why, how, and when it appears. After learning that bats navigate through echolocation, Nakisha marveled, "That's real? So cool." When Nakisha reads like a scientist, her next question will be "How do they do that?"

Water Can Be . . . (Salas) playfully presents cause and effect while focusing on the most important molecule on our planet: water. Life can't exist without it; it is a habitat, and as rain, river, and ocean, it sculpts the landscape. Water is a catalyst for so many cause-and-effect relationships in both the natural and engineered worlds. Observant readers will quickly pick up the pattern that makes this book a winner. The effect is written in word pairs, and the cause is conveyed by the illustrations. On one page, water is labeled as a "home maker" and the illustration shows jellyfish and other marine life in their ocean habitat; the opposite page offers "ship breaker" and we see a freighter caught at sea in a huge storm. In any book, you can set your students up to discover cause-and-effect relationships by using *because.* For example, water is a home maker because it provides a habitat; water is a ship breaker because it can be a big, powerful wave. (See Figure 3.4 for a beginning list of books for exploring cause and effect.)

The crosscutting concepts are intertwined, but the two heaviest threads in this science tapestry are pattern, and cause and effect. Pattern is foundational to science and cause and effect is how we understand how and why patterns and other events occur. More importantly, it is through understanding these relationships that we derive the laws and principles that govern the natural and engineered worlds. To live like a scientist is to go through life trying to understand the causes of the events we see daily. When Gil kicks an impossible goal in soccer, we might appreciate his skill, but to think like a scientist is then to ask, "How did he do that? How

Books for Cause and effect

NONFICTION	FICTION
A Tree for All Seasons (Bernard)	*Why Mosquitoes Buzz in People's Ears* (Aardema)
The Right Word: Roget and His Thesaurus (Bryant)	*Tap Tap Boom Boom* (Bluemle)
A River Ran Wild (Cherry)	*The Very Hungry Caterpillar* (Carle)
Seeds, Bees, Butterflies, and More! (Gerber)	*And Then It's Spring* (Fogliano)
It's Raining! (Gibbons)	*And the Good Brown Earth* (Henderson)
When Lunch Fights Back (Johnson)	*The Tree Lady* (Hopkins)
The Boy Who Harnessed the Wind (Kamkwamba and Mealer)	*Wind Flyers* (Johnson)
Butterflies in the Garden (Lerner)	*Baseball Saved Us* (Mochizuki)
Water Dance (Locker)	*Blackout* (Rocco)
The Noisy Paint Box: The Colors and Sounds of Kandinsky's Abstract Art (Rosenstock)	*In November* (Rylant)
Water Can Be . . . (Salas)	*The True Story of the 3 Little Pigs* (Scieszka)
First the Egg (Seeger)	*Somebody Loves You, Mr. Hatch* (Spinelli)
Rain (Stojic)	*Alexander and the Terrible, Horrible, No Good, Very Bad Day* (Viorst)
A Drop of Water (Wick)	*Farmer Duck* (Waddell)
	Each Kindness (Woodson)
	Letting Swift River Go (Yolen)

Figure 3.4
A beginning list of books for exploring cause and effect

did he utilize the laws of physics to score that goal? And how can he do it again?" To think like a scientist is to see the wonder in something as simple as a pen. What's the cause-and-effect relationship and mechanism between the ink, roller, and paper? What's the chemistry and physics that allows me to write? Is it friction (physics) or bonding between the ink and paper (chemistry)? In essence, to live and read like a scientist is to go through life acknowledging if it happens, there is a cause and a mechanism. With a little bit of curiosity, cleverness, and the right questions, we can probably figure out what it is and gain a deeper understanding of our lives, and perhaps this knowledge will help us solve a problem.

4

STRUCTURE AND FUNCTION

Appreciating the Paper Clip

Figure 4.1
The structure of the chimney serves the function of drawing the smoke away from the house.

Learning and Teaching the Science

What You Need to Know: *Structure Dictates Function*

Mark often says that he is not a handy person even though he owns a Sawzall and has used it successfully. But in his pre-Sawzall days, he enjoyed wandering the tool aisles of the local hardware store trying to figure out the purpose and use of all of the oddly shaped tools and foreign objects. Like Mark, we all deduce that this is how structure and function works—the structure of an object tells us what it does. (See Figure 4.1.)

Helping your students see structure and function relationships is a key step in developing an understanding of how things work in the world. All of us have watched young children grab a tool and intuit how to use it, but how? What are the visual clues? Watch the children in your classroom as they pick up a pair of scissors. The handle provides a visual clue of how they should interact with it and even how to use it. The same is true of a handheld hole punch. A child will very quickly deduce how to use one because the shape provides clues. One of

Mark's favorite ways to teach this idea is to give students tools—the more unorthodox the better—and have them guess the functions. More times than not they get it right, and when they discuss how they deduced the purpose of each tool, they often reveal one of the central types of cause-and-effect relationships found in science—structure dictates function.

In addition to tools, you can use familiar items such as staplers, scissors, eating utensils, and clothes hangers to lead students to the understanding that *structure dictates function*. Ask a child which utensil he or she would use to eat soup: a spoon or a fork. Why? Why do scissors cut paper but staplers don't? If you straighten a clothes hanger, does it still work? Questions like these help children see that this is how structure and function works—the structure of an object tells you what it does.

Developing Your Lens: Three Key Ideas

Shape Matters

Shape matters and the perfect place to see this is in a simple paper clip. Show your class a paper clip and ask your students to describe what it does. It is almost always easier to start the discussion by having the class define the function of the object rather than the structure. Function is typically more apparent because most of us think about *what a thing does* before *how its shape enables it*. We approach and even group objects by their function; the hardware store does not organize tools by shape, rather, tools are arranged by what they do. After your students have explained the function of the paper clip, straighten it, and ask them if it can be used to hold paper (be prepared, someone will try to jab the straightened paper clip through a stack of papers). The straightened paper clip no longer functions as it did because the shape changed. Shape dictates function.

This is the pillar of structure and function: because the structure enables the function, it is a type of cause-and-effect relationship. Objects, molecules, and life-forms come in a myriad of shapes, and the physical shape and properties of each determine what it can do and its strength and govern what it can interact with. Butterfly wings work because of their shape—they have a large surface area and are thin—which allows this insect to stay aloft by fluttering. On the other hand, airplane wings are not light nor thin but their shape creates lift when they move through the air.

Even interactions are governed by shape. Imagine you are asked to pick up a handsaw. No doubt you will grab it by the handle and not the blade simply because the shape of the grip matches your hand and the blade does not. This principle of interactions based on shape is a foundational idea in biology. Grasping tails, extended giraffe necks, canine teeth, and cockleburs only work because of their shape. We can even see how shape matters in species that interact. For example, the hummingbird's beak fits the cardinal flower's tubular shape. In many ways, this is analogous to a Phillips-head screwdriver and the matching screw—the two work together because their shapes fit and are complementary.

Physical Properties Matter

Returning to the paper clip, now use a piece of string to make the shape of a paper clip on a desktop and ask the class if this new paper clip can hold paper. This reveals the second key idea of structure and function: physical properties matter. The string may have the right shape but it is has the wrong physical properties because it is made of the wrong material.

The physical properties of a structure greatly contribute to how well it works. A paper kite can fly because it is light; one made of flattened tin cannot. Structures can be light or heavy, smooth or rough, rigid or flexible, or porous or solid, to name a few. Several years ago, Mark judged a science fair where third grader Ben tested the flying ability of paper planes made from different weights of card stock. Mark asked him what would happen if he made the same plane from a paper towel or sheet of rubber. Ben furrowed his eye brow, wrinkled his forehead, and answered with complete confidence, "Why would I do that? It wouldn't work." Clearly, the building materials help determine the success of a flying machine. The same is true of life-forms, objects, and molecules. For example, the skeleton is a supportive structure not only because of its shape but also because the minerals that serve as building blocks of the bones impart stiffness. A more dramatic example is skin. Thankfully, skin is quite elastic and it has to be, otherwise we would rip and tear every time we smiled, laughed, or even wiggled a finger. The elastic nature of skin comes from the gel-like molecules that are arranged in such a way as to allow plasticity. Understanding that shape and physical properties matter is the gateway to being able to see structure and function relationships in the biological and engineered worlds.

QUICK START FOR
Thinking About Structure and Function

To understand the relationship between structure and function, remember the two key ideas: shape matters and physical properties matter.

Ask: "What does it (object, plant or animal part) do?"

Ask: "What's its shape?"

Ask: "What are its physical properties?"

Ask: "How do the shape and physical properties enable its function?"

(See Figure 4.2.)

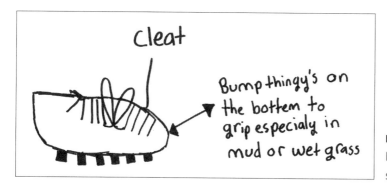

Evolution and Intent Matter

As a scientific concept, structure and function are specific to biology (the result of evolution) and engineering (the result of intentional design). Two simple questions will help your students see structure and function at work in these two worlds. In the natural world, ask, "How does this structure help this animal or plant survive or reproduce?" In the engineered world, ask, "What problem (i.e., function) was solved by the builder of this structure?"

Recognizing that structure dictates function is a critical concept for students to understand both engineering and biology. The engineered world is a good starting place because it is all around us and children have many firsthand experiences with purposefully designed and built objects. People, whether they be engineers, carpenters, or children in the Lego bin, design and then build objects to fulfill a specific function. Take, for example, two swings on a playground. The first swing is a small, bucket-shaped structure with leg holes and a harness. With no other information, the structure suggests that this swing was designed for very young children. On the other hand, a swing consisting of a wooden plank dangling from chains twenty-five feet in length calls to an older and more daring age group. Both swings were designed with intent, and at its core this is what engineering entails: solving a problem by designing the proper structure for a given function. The bucket swing holds toddlers (and excludes even the most tenacious teenager) and the plank swing is only safe for the older group.

After your students have become more adept at seeing how structure dictates function in the engineered world, they are ready to wade into the murky waters of biology. Your students may notice that we are not the only animals that build structures for a specific function; birds build nests to rear young, bees build hives to store honey and hatch offspring, and beavers build dams to create a habitat, to name a few. These animals do not engineer solutions to problems but rather these building behaviors are innate. If you discuss animal structures, you may find it helpful to explain the difference between innate behavior (e.g., beavers build dams) and learned behavior (e.g., engineers build dams). Generally, when an animal builds, it is an innate behavior that evolved to help the creature survive or reproduce. You can help students distinguish between learned and innate behaviors by asking, "Did the animal learn to build the structure or was it born knowing how to build it? If they learned it, who taught them, when, and how?"

As we pointed out earlier, the biological world was not designed but rather evolved and is much more diverse, complex, and nuanced than the engineered world. The central tenet that structure dictates function still holds true, but what makes it interesting is that the function of structures in organisms is quite specific: it's to help them either survive or reproduce. Take the moose and the beaver, both of which spend a good portion of their life in water. Ask your students to describe the shape and physical properties of the beaver's tail and the moose's legs. They both facilitate movement in the water, but how? Each has a defined shape that performs a specific function. The beaver's tail allows it to navigate quickly through the water because it is long, flat, and flexible (like a diving fin), and the moose's stiff, stilt-like legs allow it to wade through the water and graze on aquatic plants. Remember, to help your students see that the function of the tail and legs is a product of evolution, ask them, "How does each structure help the animal survive or reproduce?"

As you explore this concept with your students, consider the fact that all structure and function relationships are cause-and-effect relationships, but the reverse is not true. You may notice that some of your students start to confuse cause-and-effect relationships with structure and function. A stone in a brook may cause a ripple to form because of its shape, but the stone's function is not to make the ripple; a stone in a brook does not have a function. Evolution and intent matter, and enabling a function is a key aspect of both.

Exploring Structure and Function in Children's Literature

Structure and function appear in some books in a physically unique way, and many young children are attracted to the physical elements of books that invite them to open flaps, unfold pages, reorient the book, and open pop-ups. Diligent librarians may experience these features as attractive nuisances, but these structures often do a brilliant job at expressing ideas that typical illustrations can't deliver. When Steve Jenkins wants to convey the actual size of a snake skeleton, two gatefold pages allow him to do so. The structure of the book—extra-long pages—enables the function. The reader really gets how long the snake is. Similarly, the structure of the pop-out moon in Eric Carle's *Papa, Please Get the Moon for Me*, serves the function of contrasting the size of the moon with the father and his ladder. Your students will probably love to reminisce about lifting the flaps in board books to reveal the answers to questions or fabric swatches for tactile experiences. They may even remember patting the bunny. Flaps, gatefolds, pop-up pages, and even the book's orientation (landscape or portrait) are physical structures that authors and illustrators use for specific functions.

We can even see structure and function playing out in many genres. In the folktale *Caps for Sale* (Slobodkina), when the peddler naps with an improbably tall tower of caps on his head, it is our innate sense of structure and function that makes this humorous. Dr. Seuss and Shel Silverstein's images appeal to us for similar reasons; we know that a sidewalk doesn't "end" in the middle of nowhere, and a fish can't balance a bowling ball that is balancing a tricycle. Illustrations like these make us all laugh because they turn our sense of structure and function on its head. Whether a book shouts or whispers, you can always call attention to the shape and physical properties of different objects or animals you're discussing. Would Red Riding Hood be able to carry her basket if it were made of concrete? Could the woodsman slay the wolf with a paper axe?

Books That Shout Structure and Function

Books written specifically about structure and function, many nonfiction, are a great way for you and your students to ease into this concept because the text and illustrations are explicitly about this relationship. For example, Steve Jenkins' book *How Many Ways Can You Catch a Fly?* examines the strategies that evolved for catching flies across the animal kingdom and how different animal structures enable this same function; spiders use webs, and geckos use tongues. His book *Creature Features: 25 Animals Explain Why They Look the Way They Do* takes the opposite approach by starting with animal structures and then detailing how each does its function. On one page, Jenkins asks a hamster why its cheeks are fat (structure) and the hamster replies that it stores seeds and nuts in its cheeks (function).

Structure and function are everywhere, of course, but some topics are more accessible to children than others, and they shout this concept on seemingly every page. For students in the elementary grades, we like biology topics such as seed dispersal, pollination, animal parts like teeth and tails, and plant parts such as leaves, roots, shoots, and flowers. If you are interested in engineering, bridges, boats, airplanes, and buildings (castles!) are equally good starting points. Like Steve Jenkins, another nonfiction superstar author, Gail Gibbons, has written several books about animal features that enable unique functions, and she has also written about objects in the engineered world including skyscrapers and cameras. In books like these, the structure–function relationship is explicit and highlighted.

Book Selection and Beginning Conversations

Remember, shape matters and all picture books present objects that have shapes whether they be tails, pedals, or petals, so layering in some talk about structure and function during read-aloud is easy. The most helpful illustrations will allow you to see the connection between the shape and what the object does, like a flyswatter connecting with a fly. Start by identifying the function of the objects or the animal/plant parts in the book; next ask whether the illustrations show how the structure accomplishes this function. When you see a paintbrush, ask your students which end goes in the paint and which end in the hand and how they know. If you get stuck, try to draw parallels to the examples we have given you—screwdriver, saw, paper clip, and butterfly wings. Next, consider how the text complements or enriches this information. The best books weave visual and textual information together to build understanding. A book like *Teeth* (Collard) may show the pointy teeth of a vampire bat accompanied by the word *slice*.

To understand that physical properties matter, consider whether a structure you're discussing needs to be small, large, stiff, plastic, dense, light, or flexible to do its thing. Illustrations are key in helping readers grasp that not just any material would work, and the text often adds details and vocabulary that enrich the understanding. For example, in an illustration from *Mr. Ferris and His Wheel* (Davis), we see an enormous structure; from the text we learn that it is made of a "strong new metal called steel." We can't resist advising here to avoid books that will go over like a lead balloon.

To help you pick books that are *about* structure and function, for students at all grade levels, try the guidelines that follow (keep in mind two key ideas: *shape matters and physical properties matter*).

BOOKS ABOUT BIOLOGY

- Pick a book about a specific animal or plant part, or a specific living function. You want a book that highlights either a structure (such as tails) or function (such as pollination). Remember the whole point of shout books is to teach the reader about the structure and function relationship; some authors start with structure (*What Do You Do with a Tail Like This?* [Jenkins]) and others with function (*Flowers Are Calling* [Gray]) but all end by illuminating this relationship.

- Consider the title. You will know immediately you are on the right track with a title like *A Fruit Is a Suitcase for Seeds* (Richards), but some titles are more subtle, for instance *Aviary Wonders Inc. Spring Catalog and Instruction Manual* (Samworth). If the title hints animal and plant parts, take a look to see if it's about structure and function.

- Finally, apply the litmus test: does the book show what something does (function), what it looks like (structure), and how it does it (structure and function relationship)? For example, a book about pollination would show flowers and insects, the process of pollination, and how their respective structures allow this to occur.

BOOKS ABOUT ENGINEERING

- Consider the title. Find a book whose title suggests problem-solving or design. For example, *Mr. Ferris and His Wheel* tells the story of creating a new ride for the 1893 World's Fair. Some titles *shout* that a book is about solving an engineering problem such as *The Boy Who Harnessed the Wind* (Kamkwamba and Mealer). Similarly, it's easy to predict that David MacCaulay's *Castle* and *Mosque* or any others in this series are about these marvels of design.

- Apply the litmus test: does the book convey the problem (function)? Is it clear how the shape and physical properties of the building materials solve the problem? For example, a girl might experiment with different materials and shapes to build a kite that will fly in a strong wind.

In the following table, we present three books about biology and one about engineering to illustrate how you might guide your students to the key ideas while exploring structure and function. The questions in this table follow a clear pattern for discussing structure and function relationships that apply to any book: students identify the shape of the thing, its physical properties, and how these enable it to function. (See Figure 4.3 for a beginning list of books that shout structure and function.)

TALK PROMPTS for exploring structure and function in books that shout

Use this book to:	Notice this:	Ask this:
Introduce the concept of structure and function in the animal world	*What Do You Do with a Tail Like This?* (Jenkins) challenges readers to guess which animal parts accomplish which functions. For example, one page features different noses, and readers have to guess which animal they belong to. Why does one nose have nostrils on top (an alligator needs to breathe while mostly underwater), while another has twenty-two pink appendages? (The starry-nosed mole uses these to find its way around.) Connections between structure and function are clear to young and older readers.	• What does this nose do (function)? • Describe the nose. What is its shape? • What are the physical properties that allow this nose to dig, breathe, or spray water? • Why are the shape and physical properties key to what each nose does?

continues

Use this book to:	Notice this:	Ask this:
Introduce concept of structure and function in the plant world	*Flowers Are Calling* (Gray) is about pollination and gets the point across by offering a structure–function matching game between flower and pollinator. We see a porcupine and a hummingbird next to a trumpet honeysuckle; it's an easy guess that only the hummingbird's beak will fit inside of the long, tubular-shaped flower. Flower shape, smell, and color all "call" to the pollinator with the best matching structure.	• Describe the shape of the flower. • Describe the shape of the pollinator. • What are the physical properties (weight, size, and flexibility) of both the pollinator and the flower? • How are the shape and physical properties of both the pollinator and flower key to pollination (function)? Remember how the Phillips-head screwdriver works.
Deepen students' understanding by applying what they have learned	*Aviary Wonders Inc. Spring Catalog and Instruction Manual* (Samworth) humorously mimics a catalog featuring bird parts and invites older readers to "build their own bird" by mixing and matching feet, wings, beaks, and feathers by function. Are you designing a water bird? Buy some webbed feet. Will your bird eat fish? Buy a long pointed beak for stabbing.	These questions focus on beaks: • What do you want your bird to eat (function)? • Which of the beak shapes would enable this? • What are the physical properties of the beak that will enable it to function? Is it stiff? Hollow? Strong?
Introduce concept of structure and function in engineering	In *Mr. Ferris and His Wheel* (Davis), it's a delight to learn that the Ferris wheel came from a boy's observation of a water wheel at a mill. As an adult, Mr. Ferris used his engineering skills to design and build a huge "monster wheel" for the Chicago World's Fair in 1893.	In engineering, always start with the problem to be solved. • What is the problem or goal (the function is to build a Ferris wheel)? • What are the obstacles to building the wheel? • Describe the shape and how it carries people. • What physical properties will enable the Ferris wheel to carry people safely while rotating?

BIOLOGY

Birds: Nature's Magnificent Flying Machines (Arnold)

A Seed Is Sleepy (Aston)

The Tiny Seed (Carle)

Teeth (Collard)

Outside Your Window: A First Book of Nature (Davies)

Monarch and Milkweed (Frost)

Planting the Wild Garden (Galbraith)

Seeds, Bees, Butterflies, and More! (Gerber)

Tell Me, Tree (Gibbons)

Plant Secrets (Goodman)

Animals in Flight (Jenkins and Page)

Creature Features (Jenkins and Page)

How Many Ways Can You Catch a Fly? (Jenkins and Page)

Move! (Jenkins and Page)

Whose Teeth Are These? (Lynch)

Flip, Float, Fly: Seeds on the Move (Macken)

What If You Had Animal Teeth? (Markle)

Isabella's Garden (Millard)

Dandelions: Stars in the Grass (Posada)

A Fruit Is a Suitcase for Seeds (Richards)

Seeds (Robbins)

This Is the Sunflower (Schaefer)

Swirl by Swirl: Spirals in Nature (Sidman)

Feathers: Not Just for Flying (Stewart)

Mama Built a Little Nest (Ward)

You Nest Here with Me (Yolen and Stemple)

ENGINEERING

Building Our House (Bean)

Pop's Bridge (Bunting)

Workshop (Clements)

The Golden Gate Bridge (Doherty)

13 Bridges Children Should Know (Finger)

How a House Is Built (Gibbons)

Airplanes: Soaring! Diving! Turning! (Hubbell)

Boats: Speeding! Sailing! Cruising! (Hubbell)

The World's Most Amazing Bridges (Hurley)

Bridges: Amazing Structures to Design, Build, and Test (Johmann and Rieth)

The Boy Who Harnessed the Wind (Kamkwamba and Mealer)

Building a Bridge (Macken)

The Brooklyn Bridge: A Wonders of the World Book (Mann)

Twenty-One Elephants and Still Standing (Prince)

You Wouldn't Want to Work on the Brooklyn Bridge! An Enormous Project That Seemed Impossible (Ratliff)

Golden Gate Bridge (Riggs)

Let's Go to the Hardware Store (Rockwell)

Bridges Are to Cross (Sturges)

Queen Victoria's Bathing Machine (Whelan)

Figure 4.3

A beginning list of books that shout structure and function

Topic Spotlight: Seed Dispersal and Bridges

Seed Dispersal in a Nutshell. The role of fruit in seed dispersal is the ideal topic for introducing structure and function in the biological world because the two key ideas—shape matters and physical properties matter—are apparent and just about all students have firsthand experience with fruit. Flowering plants spread their seeds using fruit, and there are many titles that show this effectively. *Flip, Float, Fly: Seeds on the Move* (Macken) shouts the ways that the function of seed dispersal depends on the structure of the fruit. The illustrations in this book show how each type of plant uses a different type of dispersal: wind, water, animals, or flinging. Each of these methods depends on the structure of the fruit that encases the seed. For example, a bat eats the fleshy part of a fig, and then poops it out with seeds intact. The round coconut can float like a beach ball; the air inside makes it buoyant, just as floaties help children swim. Another illustration effectively shows how the spiky Velcro-like structure of seeds with burrs enables them to travel by hitchhiking on birds, animals, and human socks. Some seeds are dispersed by the wind, and the maple tree's helicopter-shaped samara is an efficient structure for this mechanism. One of the more surprising mechanisms may be how a seed pod, like lupine, dries and splits, which then flings the seeds.

Studying structure and function in any book on seed dispersal is as easy as asking:

- How does the seed travel? This is the function of the fruit.

- What's shape of the fruit? Is it round, parachute-like, long, spiky?

- What are the physical properties of the fruit? Is it heavy, flexible, light, stiff?

- How do the shape and physical properties enable the fruit to disperse its seeds? Look for responses that link the two. Burrs attach to animal fur or socks *because* they are spiky fruits.

We observed a first-grade teacher do exactly this with a book on monarchs that featured milkweed seeds drifting on the wind. When she asked how the shape and physical properties allow the seeds to travel, the students responded with ideas like, "Because the white stuff spreads like a fan or peacock. It catches the wind," and "It is like a hot air balloon. The heavy seed part is like the basket and the wind blows the white fluffy part like a balloon."

During an activity like this there is no set vocabulary; you really just want students to use words that accurately describe either the shape or the physical properties. Watch out for observations about the chemistry of fruit (smell, color, and taste), which are pattern and cause and effect (see Chapters 2 and 3), because although they attract animals to disperse the fruit, they do not affect the structure.

Remember that structure and function have a type of cause-and-effect relationship, and an effective way to help students understand this is by having them complete the sentence: "If _____, then _____." The first blank is completed with an observation about the structure followed by the effect this would have. See Figure 4.4.

Bridging to Engineering. You can't beat bridges as an engineering topic. These structures provide the opportunity to explore with your students one of the most fundamental questions of the designed world—how do we get to the other side? The possibilities are endless; the other side could be across a street, river, lake, canyon, or any other space that needs to be safely traversed. A bridge may not even be the answer—sometimes a zip line is what you really need—but that is what engineering is all about: solving a problem. If the function of a bridge is to span a space (e.g., the problem) then the engineer's job is to design the structure (e.g., the bridge) that will do this.

Figure 4.4

Marzie's pictures show that she understands structure and function

Fruit or Vegetable?

The term *fruit* is often confusing because the grocery store definition is different from the scientific one. Scientists define fruits as structures that develop from flowers and house seeds, which means that oranges, apples, squash, and peppers are all fruits—if it has a seed inside it, it is a fruit (yes, a green bean is also a fruit).

A trio of delightful picture books expertly depicts the challenges faced in completing the Golden Gate and the Brooklyn Bridges, two engineering landmarks. *Pop's Bridge* (Bunting) details the construction challenges of spanning the San Francisco Bay. Students will love the unique weight test described in the aptly titled *Twenty-One Elephants and Still Standing* (Prince). *Bridges Are to Cross* (Sturges) shouts about structure and function through impressive paper collage illustrations, captions, text, and sidebars. This engaging compendium of bridge structures will help any student see how each obstacle—river, mountain valley, busy highway—requires a carefully designed structure to cross. In one example, the island neighborhoods of Venice are connected by pedestrian bridges with steps; the structure of these bridges only has to support foot traffic. Architects of the Tower Bridge of London connected the two banks of the Thames River but also accommodated river traffic below with a drawbridge. You and your students can explore the many functions of bridges—to carry water (aqueducts), defense (castle moats), and transportation (pedestrian, car, train) with an eye to understanding the challenge that bridge builders face: what structure and materials will help them create the workable solution?

Studying structure and function in any book about bridges is as easy as asking:

- What problem does this bridge solve? This is the function.

- Who or what will cross this bridge? How do they cross—walk, drive, bike, or other method? This is part of the function; it will determine the shape and physical properties.

- What is the space like that has to be spanned by the bridge? Is it long? Deep? Windy? This will determine the shape of the bridge and what it is made of (physical properties).

- What is the shape of the bridge and what's it made of?

The age and experience of your students will determine how deep you go into various structures and why they work. Most students do not need to learn about load distribution, but they will benefit from understanding that some shapes and materials work better than others for different functions.

In addition to exploring structure and function, you might also find opportunities to talk about how bridges are universal symbols in the designed and literary worlds. They are cultural icons (London Bridge), historical turning points (General Burnside's Bridge in the Battle of Antietam), engineering marvels (Golden Gate Bridge), and literary devices (*Bridge to Terabithia* [Paterson]). Bridges span spaces both literally (the Mississippi) and metaphorically (*that's water under the bridge*). We even use the bridge metaphor to describe life decision making: *burning your bridges* and *crossing a bridge when you get to it.*

Books That Whisper Structure and Function

We typically find that books whisper about structure and function in one of two ways. Some books use the principles of this concept to resolve an aspect of the plot. For example, in the classic tale "The Three Little Pigs," each pig builds a house (same structure and function) but they change materials, which as we all know has real consequences for two of the three pigs. You could launch an interesting discussion by considering whether there would even be a story if all three pigs had chosen the same building material. In the powerful true story of *Henry's Freedom Box* (Levine), an enslaved man mails himself from Virginia to free Philadelphia. Although escaping slavery is the sobering theme of the book, Henry's successful escape hinged on constructing a box that would hold him, allow him to breathe, and protect him through his daring and arduous journey. Both of these books show how structure and function help to resolve a problem.

Other books whisper about structure and function through illustrations that reflect either evolution or intent. Playing I Spy with the illustrations in any picture book encourages students to notice incidental examples of structure and function in illustrations of everyday life. Students will begin to see these everywhere—a character carrying a basket full of picnic items for her grandmother, a stroller with a bucket seat and wheels to transport a baby brother, or a bird carrying an insect in its beak. One of our favorite activities is to choose random books and then have students, regardless of age, describe the structure and function relationships they see. We picked *Last Stop on Market Street* (Peña) off the shelf and found examples on every page: the curved handle and tentlike canopy of an umbrella, crochet hooks, eyeglasses with curved ear-pieces, windshield wipers on a bus. Even books that play with reality in their illustrations can spark a discussion about whether the structure and function relationship shown could really work. You can go deeper than I Spy if you find a book where an object plays a role in the plot. For example, in *Brave Irene* (Steig), the plucky Irene creates a sled out of a dress box to deliver a ball gown on time during a snowstorm; can you image what would have happened if she had been carrying a garment bag?

Older readers may find themselves beginning to visualize structure and function in novels; they all know that Katniss' bow is not made of papier-mâché but something much stronger that can rebound. To help your students read like scientists, invite them to describe the structures that enable characters to live in a boxcar, survive in a cave, or snare a rabbit.

Although plants and animals populate the pages of children's literature, identifying the relationship between structure and function can be a tad trickier because organisms' bodies have many functions and an illustration can only show one or two. For example, an illustration showing a bird flying in the distance tells you something about wings but not how the beak functions. Picture books are filled with images of animals and plants but the key is to ask yourself which structure and function relationship is illustrated. If we see a dog eating a bone, we may learn something about its teeth but not about how its legs help it run. On the other hand, if we see a greyhound running, we know something about its legs but not its teeth.

To get you started, we have generated for any whisper book a list of prompts that you can pose to students. To illustrate how these could play out, let's return to Steig's *Brave Irene* as an example. In this story, Irene's dressmaker mother takes ill, and Irene must deliver a beautiful gown in a raging snowstorm. To make up time, she slides down a hillside on the dress box. In this way the box (structure) is used for sledding down the hill (function).

TALK PROMPTS to help you notice structure and function in books that whisper

Prompt	How these would look in a discussion about *Brave Irene*
Choose an object in the illustrations—what is it? What is it being used for?	Irene carries the ball gown in a large protective box; it then becomes her sled.
Describe its shape. Is it big, flat, round? Is it thick or thin?	The rectangular, thin box is as tall as she is.
How does the shape enable it to do its job?	The box can become Irene's makeshift sled because it is flat, thin, and big enough to carry her.
What is it made of? Is it heavy, light? Flexible or rigid? Is the surface smooth or rough?	The box is cardboard, light, and smooth. It is rigid enough to hold its shape but flexible and smooth enough to ride the bumps in the snow.
How do these physical properties that you just described allow it to work (function)? One fun way to think about this is to ask, what if a rigid object were flexible, or a light object, heavy? Here's where the "lead balloon" joke starts to make sense.	Because the box is light, rigid, and smooth, it can slide on the snow while carrying Irene's weight, like a sled. These physical properties and shape also allow it to protect the dress throughout this wild adventure.
Was it built by humans? What problem does it solve? How do the shape and materials work together to solve the problem?	The rigid and solid sides and large shape protect the dress from the elements and keep it from wrinkling.
If it's alive (evolved), how does the shape (structure) allow the animal or plant to live (survive) or reproduce?	Because Irene's box is from the engineered world, this question doesn't apply.

Learning to read like a scientist is really about developing a lens. Once students add structure and function to their view, they see relationships in the world differently. Webbed feet and flippers say *swim fast*. Cat claws shout *tree climber* and *mouser*. Kayak says *maneuver me* and barge says *load me*. With this lens in place, structure and function appear even when you are not looking for them. This is where books that whisper are powerful, because students will now see structure and function every time they read a picture book or go to the hardware store to buy a new tool.

5

SCALE, PROPORTION, AND QUANTITY

The Goldilocks Scale

Learning and Teaching the Science

What You Need to Know: *How Big? This Big: It's All Relative*

If we were in charge of the world—or at least the K–5 curriculum—we would have called this crosscutting concept *scale is relative*. Although understanding measurements involves scale, proportion, and quantity and is integral to mathematics and to analyzing scientific data, the key idea for students in grades K–5 is that scale is relative. In science when you hear the word *scale*, your mind probably runs through several possibilities. Is *scale* the equipment for weighing specimens? The degree marks on the side of your thermometer? The relative size of something? The inch-to-mile legend on your road map? These are all legitimate uses of the word *scale*, but for understanding systems, *scale* refers to relative size. (See Figure 5.1.)

Scale is a continuum. In the center are quantities we can observe, and at the other ends are the quantities that are

Figure 5.1
Notice that Olivia has added a foot above the house, which helps us instantly realize the *scale* of the house—it is a dollhouse.

imperceptible—the really small (size of an atom, speed of a glacier, and time it takes for an atom to decay) and the really large (size of the Milky Way, speed of light, and age of our solar system). The continuum starts with the really small (microscopic), proceeds through the middle (macroscopic, or what humans can observe), and ends in the really large (astronomical). Measurements in the middle range become second nature to us because this is where our senses operate.

One way to think of human senses is as instruments that are constantly taking measurements. When we touch the running water to see if it is hot, we're taking a measurement. Our ears are the instruments that tell us to turn up the volume on our MP3 players. Daily firsthand experiences with all of our instruments help us develop a sense of time, space (volume), temperature, and sound, to name a few. When we hear that class ends in an hour or that art class will start in twenty minutes, we know what to expect because this type of measurement is familiar to us. On the other hand, none of us have firsthand experience with 4.5 million years or a nanosecond, but scientists have developed ways to measure and understand these larger and smaller quantities.

We take and interpret measurements in the observable middle range every day. There are clocks in our schools, speedometers in our cars, and numbers on our thermostats. Administrators measure attendance, cafeteria chefs measure the amount of salt in the food, and students measure the time until recess. All measurements implicitly answer a question:

How many students are in school today?

How much salt do I need to add to my recipe?

How soon is recess?

The answer a measurement provides is only meaningful if we know the scale, quantity, and units of what is being measured. If a student says, "I can't wait for my birthday. It's in eight," we really don't know when the birthday is. Add the units (hours, days, weeks, or months) and we know instantly when to make a card; we know where we are on the scale. Units actually tell us what was measured. When we hear the terms *minute*, *miles per hour*, or *degrees*, we know that time, speed, and temperature were measured.

To understand a measurement is to know where it resides on what we affectionately call the "Goldilocks scale": is it big, little, or in the middle? To begin exploring this concept, ask your students if they would each rather have six donuts or six pennies. They will almost certainly choose six donuts. Why? Because six donuts on the donut scale is a much larger quantity than six pennies on a monetary scale. Or as fourth grader Jennifer explained, "Six pennies is worthless compared to six donuts."

The Missing Units Game

You probably already teach your students about the importance of units, but a fun way to support their learning is by playing the missing unit game. Have students imagine what units might sensibly complete entertaining and vague statements such as:

"Please water the plant with seven . . ."

"At recess I want everyone to run two . . ."

"We'll have a chance to share your great stories at the open house in three . . ."

Measurements produce quantities of units (6 ounces, 98.6 degrees, or 26.2 miles), and scale is how we understand the relative size of that measurement. Six ounces is a small cup of coffee but a lot of hot sauce, 98.6 degrees is a normal body temperature but a hot summer day in New England, and 26.2 miles is a long way to run but a short distance to drive. The operative word for understanding scale is *relative*. When Goldilocks tried each chair and found them to be either too big, too little, or just right, the sizes were relative to Goldilocks.

For example, take 122 degrees Fahrenheit. If your classroom was that temperature, you'd cancel school because it is relatively hot. If your oven was 122 degrees, you wouldn't try to bake in it. It is relatively cool. To understand a measurement is to have a feel for what is being measured and the relative position of this quantity on its scale; that's why kids will always take the donuts over the pennies. When comparing their options, they quickly realize that six donuts is a gourmand's dream but six pennies will not even fill one wallet. This is the key idea of scale: *big, little, or in the middle is relative.* That's why third grader Kyle said, "For me that's a long time, but not for the continent," after he learned that continents move over millions of years. To think like a scientist is to develop fluency in measurements and an innate feel for quantities and units on their respective scales.

Developing Your Lens: Comparisons Help Us Understand the Scale

As teachers we like the phrase *making the strange familiar,* but in this case being familiar is not good enough. To use measurements effectively, we need a deep understanding of the units

Betty Crocker's Secret

Have you ever tried to quadruple the recipe of your favorite baked dish for a large party? We bet it didn't turn out the same because the volume-to-cook-time ratio changes as volume increases—the proportion is not scalable. Betty Crocker knows this; that's why she puts tables on the back of her cake mix boxes showing recommended baking time and temperature depending on the size of your pan. On the playground, we have ruefully observed that many kids can swing on the monkey bars but few adults can. What's up with this? As we grow (let's say 10 percent), the strength required to move our weight increases by a lot more than 10 percent. Strength-to-weight ratios, like baking, are not scalable.

and what a quantity means on its relative scale (thirty-five miles per hour is fast on a bike but slow in a car). Ideally, we want to respond to a measurement without doing a mental calculation, just as we automatically slow down when the speed limit goes from thirty-five to fifteen miles per hour near a school. Those units and quantities for which we have a sense (e.g., six donuts is a lot) allow us to comprehend and react without having to ask, "Is that a big amount or small amount?"

Adults have developed an enduring understanding of quantity and units and their relative importance, and these have become second nature. We all know ten minutes is not a long commute but it's a long time to hold your breath. If we hear on the radio that the weather is sunny and seventy-five, we know how to dress. Children, on the other hand, are still developing this familiarity and are helped when they hear adjectives connected to quantities and units. In the morning before getting dressed, seven-year-old Asha asks her parents, "Hot or cold?" When told, "It's cold; it's thirty-seven degrees," Asha knows how to dress and has gotten a better sense of the temperature scale. Qualifying adjectives and statements with words that convey relativity, like *big*, *heavy*, or *fast*, can be helpful in developing a feel for units and quantity. If a third grader says, "I need help picking this up, it's heavy," we might respond, "It _is_ heavy. It weighs thirty-five pounds, which is a lot for an eight-year-old." Notice how we qualified the statement with "which is a lot for an eight-year-old." Comparisons help us understand the scale and also that a lot or a little is always relative.

You will find that most measurements you encounter are either time or size. Of these two, the one that may need immediate clarification is *size*. Although most of us usually use size to refer to volume, scientists also use it to refer to how big or little any measurement is. This is why we may refer to the speed of light as *large*—it is a big number.

Big, Little, or in the Middle? Using the Goldilocks Scale

Remember, the K–5 curriculum focuses on the macroscopic or observable scale.

Scale	Microscopic	Macroscopic (observable)	Astronomical	Microscopic	Macroscopic (observable)	Astronomical
	Relatively speaking, small can be			Relatively speaking, large can be		
Volume	A molecule	A sip of coffee	Earth	A cell	Thermos of coffee	Solar system
Weight (Mass)	An atom	A feather	The Moon	A protein	An elephant	Jupiter
Speed	A slow-moving glacier	A crawling snail	Earth orbiting	An electron spinning	A cheetah running	Light traveling
Time	A split second is a short time for an atom to exist.	A minute is a small time to wait.	A century is a short time in Earth's history.	A second is a long time for molecules to interact.	A century is a long time to live (or wait).	A million years is a long time in Earth's history.

Just remember, everything on this chart is relative! A cheetah running is slow compared to an airplane. A thermos of coffee is small if we're serving a room full of people. And if you're looking at the whole Milky Way, our solar system is really not so big after all.

Making the Imperceptible Perceptible—Even Toilet Paper Can Be a Scale Model

Comparisons are pretty straightforward when we are in the macroscopic scale. A fourth-grade runner may be fast on a scale of her peers, but slow in a race with a member of the high school varsity cross-country team. Being fast is relative. But when we find ourselves studying the really small or really large, it is trickier because we have no firsthand experience in these realms. No one has traveled at the speed of light, after all.

Analogies can help us comprehend scale because they are tangible. Louise Leakey, a world-renowned anthropologist, uses a roll of toilet paper to help us understand how long humans have been around. If Earth forms in the first sheet, then life begins at sheet 160, and dinosaurs appear at 381 and go extinct in the 395th sheet. Humans appear in the last two millimeters of sheet 400 on the roll (the last 200,000 years). This analogy with toilet paper works because we can visualize it and even touch it and the perspective helps us grasp the imperceptible. With a little imagination, you can use space to help students understand relative scale in all sorts of ways. For example, you might use your school hallway to model the relative scale of the solar system in proportionately correct intervals. It's a long walk from Earth to Pluto (even though it is not a planet). Transforming the large scale of the solar system (millions of miles) to a tangible scale (the hallway) helps children understand the distances between planets on their own scale.

QUICK START FOR
Developing Habits of Mind About Scale

Understanding scale is about asking "Big, little, or in the middle?" for any measurement. Comparisons help us understand scale. A microbe is small compared to a human but huge compared to an atom. A star is large compared to a planet but tiny compared to a galaxy. How big is the sun? As big as 1.3 million Earths.

To determine where something is on its scale, ask: "What's being measured? Time, volume, speed, weight?" Use a comparison to understand if the measurement is big, little, or in the middle. You might try the following steps:

• Pick a familiar reference point like a marker, chair, or even school bus depending upon what you are measuring.

• Determine how your subject compares to your reference point on the scale. Use phrases like, "Is it bigger, smaller, heavier, faster, the same as (the reference point)?"

You Work in a Scale Model

You can see relative scale throughout your school because just about every elementary school is a scale model of the adult world. What seems small to adults is *just right* to students. You might bring this to your students' attention by asking them to compare chairs, water fountains, toilets, and the placement of coat hooks at their school to those at the high school or other public places. Much of the school is scaled to them. Direct a thirsty fifth grader to the kindergarten water fountain and relative size is instantly relevant.

Exploring Scale in Children's Literature

Books That Shout Scale

Scale shouts differently in fiction and nonfiction. As we noted above, the key to understanding relative size is through comparisons, and in fiction where the story revolves around scale, it's easy to see. Although not a children's book, many of us are familiar with *Gulliver's Travels* (Swift) and the way the main character experiences relativity of scale when he travels as an average man in England, a giant in Lilliput, and a midget in Brobdingnag. We encounter scale comparison as plotlines in other classic novels and chapter books such as *The Borrowers* (Norton), where Arrietty and Pod hang postage stamps as pictures and use pins for knitting needles. With these objects, it's clear that size is relative; a human person's matchbox is a Borrower's storage trunk. In Wonderland, Alice becomes disconcertingly large and then small, compared to her usual state. And we all know that the size of James' peach is important so it can accommodate the equally oversized anthropomorphized insects; the magic green capsules (the mechanism!) allow James to interact with these other characters on the same scale.

Many picture books play with scale as a part of the plot. Any dollhouse book—we like *The Tub People* (Conrad)—communicates the size of the main characters by comparisons with the familiar human scale, such as the bar of soap becoming a boat. David Wiesner and Chris Van Allsburg's imaginative fantasy worlds invite us to consider what adventures can take place when we are small enough to fly on leaves, *Free Fall,* or shrink to the scale of the board game, *Jumanji.*

Fairy tale magic may take the form of enhancing scale: seven league boots enable you to take much longer strides in pursuit of villains. A beanstalk on magic steroids grows high enough for Jack (or Kate) to climb to the clouds, and a pumpkin can grow the size of a coach with a swish of a magic wand. All of these play with scale in a manner that may be charming, delightful, or preposterous to achieve their purposes and resolve the story.

Nonfiction, however, is where scale really shines, and Steve Jenkins, April Pulley Sayre, David Macaulay, and Gail Gibbons, among others, will become your go-to authors for picture books that present scale in accessible and engaging ways. Skilled authors deftly use comparisons to help readers develop a feel for units through comparisons. Jenni Desmond, in her stunning book *The Blue Whale,* uses familiar units like bicycles, trucks, vans, cars, and children to convey the length of a blue whale. On one page, we see a huge pile of fifty-five hippopotami as the comparative unit for the whale's weight. In *Just a Second: A Different Way to Look at Time,* Steve Jenkins presents events that occur in a given span of time. As you move through a second, a minute, an hour, and a day, children learn what can happen in each unit.

Book Selection and Beginning Conversations

Effective nonfiction authors use an extensive toolbox of visual strategies to show us relative size. Look for features that convey scale in the illustrations such as scale diagrams, scale models, and close-ups. Comparisons with familiar references—like a tree or an adult—are another common and effective tool deliberately used by illustrators to convey scale. In fiction, keep your eye out for stories that play with scale by increasing or decreasing the size of the characters or setting (dollhouse books like *The Tub People* and imaginary worlds like *Jumanji*).

As you search for books that shout scale, make the titles work for you. Look for titles that contain a comparison such as *too many* or hint at one end of the scale or another. When you see a title like *In the Tall, Tall Grass* (Fleming), *How Much Is a Million?* (Schwartz), *The Great Big Enormous Turnip* (Tolstoy), or *The Little House* (Burton), there is a good chance that scale is central to the book. (See Figure 5.2 for a beginning list of books that shout scale and comparison.)

TALK PROMPTS for exploring relative scale and comparison in books that shout

Use a book like this to:	Notice:	Ask:
Show how comparative illustrations in nonfiction help us conceptualize relative size on a scale.	In *Bones: Skeletons and How They Work*, Steve Jenkins cleverly helps us conceptualize the relative size of animals—including humans—through proportional comparisons of each animal's skeleton. When not shown as actual size, an author's note indicates the scale we should use, as in "Skeletons shown one-twelfth actual size."	On any page, ask, "What do you see that is familiar?" This is the reference point. Follow with, "How does it compare to the other animal skeletons? Is it big, little, or in the middle?" If you want to consider proportion, ask, "If these skeletons were actual size, how big would they be?" Use a comparison from the classroom.
Show how fiction can convey big, little, or in the middle on a scale.	The daughter in Eric Carle's *Papa, Please Get the Moon for Me* is so enamored of the moon that her father makes gallant efforts to reach it for her. He fetches an extremely long ladder and perches it on top of a tall mountain. We know the moon is big because it can't even fit on a regular page. What makes this book fun is that on a relative scale, the moon is large and far away. In a literal sense, the father can't get it for his daughter, although he tries.	Using the reference points in the illustrations such as the "very long ladder," ask, "On the big, little, or in the middle scale, how do you know the moon is big?" Illustrations like the gatefold pages show an extended ladder atop a tall mountain, which shouts that the moon is both very big and far away compared to the father and daughter.

continues

Use a book like this to:	Notice:	Ask
Explore how proportion helps us understand size on a scale. This type of nonfiction is for older (grades 3–5) readers.	*If the World Were a Village* (Smith) proportionally shrinks the human population to a village that contains one hundred members. By scaling the population from greater than 7.3 billion (an imperceptible number) to a familiar number (one hundred), readers can instantly understand language, literacy, and electricity. In this village, thirty-nine people are under the age of nineteen (approximately 2,854,020,000).	For each category presented (religion, nationality, food, and others) ask, "What's being measured?" Categories show the proportion of people with a certain religion, nationality, or diet, among others. Use the global village to compare the relative size of any given demographic, asking, "Is the proportion big, little or in the middle?" As always, choose a reference point. Students may be intrigued by comparing themselves with members of the global village.

NONFICTION

One Small Place in a Tree (Brenner)

Tiny Creatures: The World of Microbes (Davies)

The Blue Whale (Desmond)

Actual Size (Jenkins)

Biggest, Strongest, Fastest (Jenkins)

Hottest, Coldest, Highest, Deepest (Jenkins)

Just a Second (Jenkins)

Prehistoric Actual Size (Jenkins)

Born to Be Giants: How Baby Dinosaurs Grew to Rule the World (Judge)

Wilma Unlimited: How Wilma Rudolph Became the World's Fastest Woman (Krull)

FICTION

Zoom (Banyai)

Sam and Dave Dig a Hole (Barnett)

The Little House (Burton)

Papa, Please Get the Moon for Me (Carle)

The Five-Dog Night (Christelow)

The Tub People (Conrad)

James and the Giant Peach (Dahl), older readers

In the Tall, Tall Grass (Fleming), younger readers

In the Small, Small Pond (Fleming), younger readers

The Man Who Walked Between the Towers (Gerstein)

Figure 5.2

A beginning list of books that shout scale and comparison

NONFICTION (*continued*)

Cathedral: The Story of Its Construction and others in this series (Macaulay)

Material World: A Global Family Portrait (Menzel and Mann)

How Big Is a Foot? (Myller)

Guess What Is Growing Inside This Egg (Posada)

Vulture View (Sayre)

Lifetime: The Amazing Numbers in Animal Lives (Schaefer)

How Much Is a Million? (Schwartz)

If the World Were a Village (Smith)

How Big Is Big? How Far Is Far? (Sohlke-Lennert)

FICTION (*continued*)

Waiting (Henkes), for younger readers

Inch by Inch (Lionni)

The Lady and the Spider (McNulty)

The Borrowers or any in that series (Norton), older readers

Are We There Yet? (Santat)

Horton Hears a Who (Seuss)

The Great Big Enormous Turnip (Tolstoy)

Jumanji (Van Allsburg)

Flotsam (Wiesner)

Free Fall (Wiesner)

Quick as a Cricket (Wood)

Figure 5.2 (*continued*)

Topic Spotlight: Supersize Me

In the elementary classroom, size is a perfect topic for exploring the idea that scale is relative. The natural and engineered worlds are filled with marvels that are beyond our ability to perceive because they're off the human scale. No matter how fast we count, it's hard to grasp just how many times a hummingbird can flap its wings (fifty times per second!) but when compared to a gnat (250 times per second!), a hummingbird is a pretty slow flapper.

Steve Jenkins is the master of comparisons, and he has a particular genius for providing us with comparisons that help us develop a feel for actual size. Many of his books—such as *Actual Size*; *Biggest, Strongest, Fastest*; *Just a Second*; *Prehistoric Actual Size*; and *Hottest, Coldest, Highest, Deepest*—are filled with recognizable comparisons that provide opportunities to explore scale. We all know that the Empire State Building is a really tall building, so it works as a familiar reference point for many of us. In his captivating book *Hottest, Coldest, Highest,*

Figure 5.3
Nola's drawing of a large fish

Deepest, Jenkins uses this familiar reference to help us understand just how deep the Mariana Trench in the Pacific Ocean is—twenty-nine times the size of the Empire State Building. On another page we learn how extreme the rise and fall of the tide at the Bay of Fundy is through a comparison to a six-foot human's height. The sea level rises and falls nine times the height of a human every day. We are awed by these sizes precisely because the comparisons enable us to comprehend the scale. To communicate like a scientist is to use familiar references to help your audience understand the size of something. Nola shows the size of the fish she caught in a very Steve Jenkinesque way (Figure 5.3).

Books That Whisper Scale

Seeing Scale in Illustrations

Regardless of genre, any illustration can be a place to notice and talk about scale; after all, unless illustrators are graffiti or mural artists, almost all of their work has to be drawn on a smaller scale. Books are rarely life-size, which is why gatefolds (folded pages), scales, and artistic features are useful tools. Illustrators convey information like distance and size using familiar reference points drawn to scale. Readers intuitively use these references to figure out how far, close, big, or small something is. The scale references tell us what scale we are operating on, and this is implicitly communicated to us in picture books. People are the most familiar reference point, and when they're pictured, we automatically understand the scale presented in the illustration. When we see a family eating dinner, a child on the playground, or a parent pushing a stroller on the sidewalk, we know that this is a human scale (macroscopic). But adding a floor-to-ceiling cat face in the background to any of these would tell us that these people are tiny enough to live in a dollhouse world. This is how illustrators communicate a change in scale; they add a familiar reference point so we immediately understand that the perspective—or scale—has changed.

Part of the power of scale is that it can help you learn something about unfamiliar objects. If you've never seen an ostrich, an illustration of this huge bird next to a person will help you learn something about its size immediately. You might explore this comparative strategy with students by finding an illustration that allows you to compare a familiar feature with the size of another. For example, in *Flip, Float, Fly: Seeds on the Move* (Macken), an illustration shows tumbleweeds with a prairie dog in the foreground. You might cover the prairie dog and ask how big the tumbleweeds are. If you've never seen a tumbleweed, it's impossible to know unless you see the tumbleweeds in comparison to the prairie dog. Once you do, the scale is clear; the tumbleweeds are about twice the size of the prairie dog. This works in reverse for the reader who is familiar with the scale of a tumbleweed but has never seen a prairie dog. To read like a scientist is to see the relative scale in an illustration by finding what's familiar. In the context of a read-aloud, ask your students how they know the scale. Covering the clues and then revealing them can often provide that aha moment.

Scale can play a role in plot development and setting, and this is often apparent in the illustrations. Changes in scale shown through illustrations might signal that something is happening in the plot. In *The Gardener* (Stewart), when Lydia Grace moves from her family farm—a large-scale garden—to the city, the illustrations help us see that the scale and type of gardening she can do has changed and this will take some getting used to. The family's rural farm dwarfs her urban rooftop container garden, but this contrast is the challenge that she overcomes, allowing us to see Lydia Grace for the plucky gardener she is no matter the scale of her garden. Plots are often influenced by scale like the passage of time, the scope of a hero's quest, or the size of the giant's teeth. First grader Zander knows the importance of scale in telling his story about a giant cat as we can see in his illustration in Figure 5.4. Notice how scale immediately suggests where this story might be headed.

Figure 5.4
Zander uses scale to create the drama in his story.

Listening for Scale in the Language

Readers often encounter comparisons and relative terms in all kinds of texts. You can help students notice how comparisons and idioms show scale and add to our understanding and aesthetic experience as we read. Poetry is a great place to start. In *Forest Has a Song* (VanDerwater), we love the two lines that describe a fossil's place on the geological scale: "Alive for an eye blink / forever dead calm." In this case, *forever* refers to the geological scale, and *eye blink* describes the ephemeral existence of the creature on this scale.

Taking precise measurements is an important practice in science, but in everyday life we often use familiar comparisons to tell us where we are on the relative scale. If we're told, "It is going to rain cats and dogs," we know to bring an umbrella, but learning that it's going to rain an inch an hour is not as meaningful to most of us. In *Wilma Unlimited* (Krull), the true story of Olympic runner Wilma Rudolph, the crowd encourages her with "thundering cheers," which instantly answers the question, how loud? Decibels would also answer how loud, but would not tell us as clearly that the crowd is on her side.

Our culture is filled with idioms and similes that wink at measurement and scale. *Blink of an eye*, *faster than lightning*, *speed of light* are phrases we use to convey *it's really fast*. On the other end of the scale, we indicate slowness with phrases like *snail's pace*, *glacially slow*, and *slower than molasses*. To read like a scientist is to recognize that this use of language is a way to communicate scale. You might ask, "What does the comparison help you understand? How does the comparison tell you what is being measured? Why is this an effective comparison?" Here is a list of some of our favorite comparisons that help us determine where we are on a particular scale:

TIME

Blink of an eye

Faster than lightning

Glacially slow

It's light years away

Not in my lifetime

Not on my watch

Older than the hills

Snail's pace

Slo-mo

Slower than molasses

Speed of light

Time stood still

When hell freezes over

TEMPERATURE

Cold as ice

Freezing cold

Hot as hell

Like being baked in an oven

Lava hot

Stone cold

Three-dog night

WEIGHT (MASS)

Heavier than a lead brick

Heavier than a lead zeppelin

Lighter than air

Lighter than a feather

VOLUME

Bigger than a breadbox

Bigger than a house

Small as a speck of dust

Small enough to fit on a pinhead

Smaller than a pea

SOUND

Loud and clear

Loud as thunder

Loud enough to wake the dead

Quiet as a mouse

Could hear a pin drop

Consider adding to this list with your students as they read throughout the year. You could even make a relative scale based on these phrases. There are no absolute right answers, but having your students discuss the placement of these on a continuum requires that they consider the power and meaning in each comparison. We're still arguing over which is quieter—a mouse or a pin drop!

As we made this list, we noticed that these phrases describe the extremes of the Goldilocks scale—really hot, really cold, really fast, or really slow. Phrases describing the middle of the scale, or the realm of just right, are conspicuously absent. We racked our brains (another measurement) and the only idioms or similes we could find that refer to the middle are *same old-same old (so-so)* and *middle of the road*.

Remember pattern? The middle range is the typical pattern we expect and our language reflects this. When we hear the weather report, "It's going to be a typical summer day," we know what to expect because it's a known pattern. We use language to convey a change in what we expect—a break in the pattern. A phrase like "Tomorrow it's going to be hot enough to cook an egg on the sidewalk" tells us that tomorrow is going to be unusually hot for us here in Vermont. We are all pattern spotters and so we are already aware of the normal range of the scales of our daily lives, such as temperature and length of day. Remember *normal* is just another way to say *pattern*. You already know what the typical weather is for your location; you have a feel for what is just right. Language has evolved to help us communicate when the pattern is changing on the relative scale.

Not everything we measure is quantifiable by science, and every culture has come up with its own delightful comparisons, which are quite clear to the listener. You know to stay away from a colleague when you hear that today he is *prickly as a porcupine* but instead approach him when he is as *happy as a lark*. Even though we really don't know the emotional state of a lark, this simile makes its point clearly. During read-aloud, you might watch for idioms and similes that refer to an atypical scale. Although these figures of speech won't help students develop scientific understandings per se, they do raise awareness of the *idea* of scale in language and thought.

In the following table, we explore how both language and illustrations can help your students develop a sense of scale and how understanding scale is what makes each of these books work. First we highlight language use in Eileen Spinelli's book, *Heat Wave*. Notice how her language choices convince us just how hot it is. Even though cold showers are not standard units, your students can imagine how hot it is when one character complains it is a *four cold-shower* day. Next, we examine how scale helps us understand the ideas presented through illustrations in *Guess What Is Growing Inside This Egg* (Posada). The prompts we present can be applied to any book that whispers scale. (See Figure 5.5 for a beginning list of books that whisper scale.)

TALK PROMPTS for helping students see how language whispers scale

Prompts for noticing how language and comparisons convey scale	How these would look in a discussion about *Heat Wave* (Spinelli)
Remember adjectives, comparisons, idioms, and similes can hint at measurement. Ask, "What does the language suggest is being measured?" Next, ask, "Is it big, little, or in the middle?" Help students realize that authors convey relative size through word choice by asking, "How do we know it is big, little, or in the middle? What words tell us?"	Because this book is about a heat wave, we know that temperature is being measured. Ask, "How hot is it and how do we know?" We know it is really hot because of adjectives like *sizzle* and *frizzled*. Comparisons and descriptions also tell us it is hot: *four cold showers* and *Ralphie forgot about the lemonade and just sold ice.*

TALK PROMPTS for helping students see how illustrations whisper scale

Prompts for noticing how illustrations convey relative scale through reference points	How these would look in *Guess What Is Growing Inside This Egg* (Posada)
Have your students identify the main subject in an illustration (i.e., what it is about). Ask, "What clues tell you if the subject is big, little, or in the middle? Where does it fall on the scale? Is the subject a close-up, actual size, or zoomed out?"	This book shows eggs from different animals. We see a giant egg nearly filling up the whole page, but we understand the scale—it is actual size—when we see the penguin toes that are supporting the egg. On another page, we see a large egg and understand that we have zoomed in when we see relatively giant spider legs next to it. For each page you might ask, "Is the egg big, little, or in the middle?" Follow up with, "How do you know? What are the clues that you used as a comparison to determine the relative size?"

Eggs 1, 2, 3: Who Will the Babies Be? (Halfmann)

My Friend Whale (James)

Henry Hikes to Fitchburg (Johnson)

All the Water in the World (Lyon)

Roxaboxen (McLerran)

Kate and the Beanstalk (Osborne)

Guess What Is Growing Inside This Egg (Posada)

Our Stars (Rockwell)

Stars Beneath Your Bed: The Surprising Story of Dust (Sayre)

Heat Wave (Spinelli)

Forest Has a Song (VanDerwater)

Figure 5.5

A beginning list of books that whisper scale

Initially, we weren't sure how this concept would be useful to elementary students. Then we remembered that even Goldilocks used measurement and scale to make herself comfortable; she had developed a second nature for what was just right. Like Goldilocks, to live like a scientist is to develop an enduring understanding of the units, quantities, and relative size of measurements (you might even say that to eat like a scientist is to choose the six donuts). Great picture books offer an opportunity to nimbly move between a visual representation of size and comparisons found in language. If the goal is to make measurement second nature, you're all set; you're surrounded with picture books that are—by their very nature—scale models.

6

SYSTEMS AND SYSTEM MODELS

Life in a Fishbowl

Learning and Teaching the Science

What You Need to Know: *Use Pattern to Define a System*

Coincidentally, we go to the same dentist (not at the same time) and for years have admired the glass terrarium in the waiting room. In this teardrop-shaped ecosystem are plants, soil, water, and microbes. Adding only indirect light and ambient temperature, this miniature world works: the gases cycle with the help of the plants and microbes, water moves from the soil into the plants and back into the enclosed atmosphere, and, in the end, the plants grow. Our dentist's terrarium is a system with *components* (water, gases, plants, soil, and microbes) that *interact* (cause and effect) within a *boundary* (the glass wall) and energy in the form of light and heat flows through the whole entity. (See Figure 6.1.)

What is a system? The vocabulary used to describe systems is a bit clunky, but the idea of a system is really straightforward. A system is anything that consists of interacting components

Figure 6.1

The house in the drawing is a perfect example of a system with boundaries and interacting components (walls, roof, floor). We can view this system as a dollhouse or as a model for larger houses.

within a boundary, and in fact, every object can be considered a system. Systems can be really simple like a ball or stapler, or they can be complex like a cell or ecosystem. How do we know a system when we see one? The key is to identify the boundaries and the interacting components that define the system.

How do we know a stapler is a system? Because it's a whole thing that has a boundary (we can touch and see where the stapler begins and ends) and it has interacting components (springs, levers, and staples). How do we know a cell is a system? It has a boundary (the membrane) and interacting components (the stuff inside). We might not think of a soccer ball as a system, but let's put it to the test. Does it have a boundary and interacting components? Yes. Because we can hold the ball, we recognize that it must have a boundary and that it is made of "stuff" that works together. When pressed to explain *stuff*, we might point out that the stitches, octagons, valve, and air interact in this system. To think like a scientist is to see the boundaries and interacting components that make up any system. How the components interact determines what the system does, and these cause-and-effect interactions are what we measure and observe to help us understand the system.

All systems are defined by a pattern and the key to identifying any system is to spot the boundary and interactions that make up the pattern. We all know a bridge, tree, and dog when we see one because we know the pattern that defines these systems. We know where each of them begins and ends (the structural boundary) and what each system does (function or behavior). For example, if we focus on a dog, the structural boundary is the soft fur and what this system does is bark, run, wag, and eat.

To help your students develop the habit of mind of seeing systems, you might consider picking up objects (systems) in your classroom and asking your students to identify the pattern that defines the system. Ask, "Where does the pen begin and end? What does the pen do?" The pen's shape forms its boundary, and its interacting components like the ball and ink enable it to write. Objects are a great entry point and they will start your students down the path to understanding that systems are defined by their patterns.

As you move into more complex systems, the defining boundaries and behaviors may be more fluid. Take a desert ecosystem, for instance. It has a spatial boundary and defining characteristics (hot and dry), but both of these fall along a continuum; there is no magic line to step over to leave the desert. Systems with murky boundaries are defined by the people who study the system. Where does the desert end? Along this ten-mile transition zone where the temperature and water change.

Systems can be categorized as either open or closed. In closed systems, the components interact with each other but nothing goes in and nothing goes out; that is, no energy or matter is added or lost from the system. In open systems, matter and energy flow through the system.

Stuff comes in and stuff goes out. Our favorite closed system is a thermos of hot chocolate. Once we pour in the hot chocolate, the thermos is a closed system because no energy is lost as heat because it is surrounded by a vacuum and because no molecules of hot chocolate escape until we open it. On the other hand, like most systems, our dentist's terrarium is an open system because light passes through the glass and heat is gained or lost.

Systems in the engineered world deserve a special shout-out because engineered systems are always defined by structure (spatial boundary) and function. Remember, this is what engineers do—they create systems with a structure that achieves a specific function. Pick up the stapler. It's a system made of interacting components, and its structure was designed to wrangle a pile of loose papers into a tidy stapled stack. We define this system by its structure and the fact that it does a certain function. If a papier-mâché object looked like a stapler, we wouldn't call it a stapler because it wouldn't work. The function is essential to the system.

Social systems are defined by the relationship (pattern) of the interacting components. Take a flock of geese. How do we know one when we see one? Because the flock is flying south in a *V* formation, honking. The flock is a system made up of interacting geese but because the flock moves around we can't define the boundary spatially; instead it is defined by the relationship of the components. When a goose gets lost during migration it is no longer part of its flock (the system) because it is no longer interacting with the other birds. Social systems like a community, sports team, or herd of animals are defined by social interactions that create an abstract boundary. We might think of the expression *getting voted off of the island* as meaning *you have been asked to leave this system*. Unfortunately, we have all seen this on the playground as children are inclusive or exclusive in their play. When children create cliques, they are establishing systems based on relationships.

Many of your students may quickly realize that there are systems within systems. To help your students see this, you might have them write their address as name, street, town, state, zip code, United States of America, North America, Earth, Solar System, and finally Universe. The point of this task is to illustrate that there are systems within systems. By changing scale, we can see that the interacting components of any system are systems themselves. If we go back to the dog, we know it is a system but the dog is also made of smaller systems like the circulatory system, nervous system, cells, and organs. Even the easel in your classroom is made of subsystems like the screws, hinges, brace, marker tray, and paper. So what's the difference between a system and interacting components? Scale. As shown by the clever address activity, every component can be a system itself if the scale is changed. Your home and street are systems, but they are also components within the much larger scale of the Earth system.

To understand a complex system, scientists often consider each component individually as a system. It's sort of like tackling a big problem by solving the smaller ones first. This is what scientists do when they study the heart or liver to better understand human health. The system may be the human body, but given its complexity, scientists pick boundaries to divide it into more accessible subsystems.

To think like a scientist is to study the proverbial trees to understand the forest. Just as you set boundaries in your classroom for behavior (your classroom is a system), as a scientist you set the boundaries of the system you wish to study and your questions tell you where to place those boundaries. If you wanted to investigate the effects of photosynthesis, your system might be a terrarium, an entire ecosystem, or even the Earth, but if you were interested in the *mechanisms* of photosynthesis you would probably choose just the leaf or chloroplast as your system.

Developing Your Lens: Three Ideas for Understanding Systems and System Models

Models Are Like Mini-Mes That Help Us Understand the Larger System

A useful strategy for understanding systems is to create a model of the system. Any time your school holds a fire drill, you are using a model to ask, "What if there was a fire?" Would all of the students reach the playground safely? If the route for your fire drill means you are colliding with other classes, you plan a different route. The model allows you to see how things might go in a true emergency, which then allows you to change the exit route. A rehearsal of how your students will host visitors during the science fair allows them a dry run, or a chance to ask: "What if someone asks me to explain my experiment?" Modeling how a system might work allows us to make changes in a safe arena.

Children build models every time they play with blocks, Legos, or Minecraft. Their imagined worlds are representations of systems. After building houses for her Superman figure, third grader Rae explained that only certain roof shapes work. Rae modeled houses until she created one that worked. Just as scientists manipulate variables in their models, children manipulate the components of their models. A model is the tool that helps us conceptualize what happens in the system and how it happens (mechanism!). This is why a physical therapist pulls out a plastic model of a knee when talking to patients.

Modeling is how we represent what we know, and we can use the predictions we make based on models to test our current understanding of a system. Ask fifth graders to diagram the fate of their breakfast, and this will reveal their understanding of the digestive system. Ask a gastrointestinal doctor to draw the same model and it will look very different; each model represents the knowledge of its creator. In ten years, ask these same students to update their models and they will very likely be more detailed. Modeling is useful in science and engineering because it helps us conceptualize complex systems. How does a human heart work? You can't see your heart but the beat reassures you that it is there when taking a peek is not easy. A model, whether it be a diagram, computer simulation, or 3-D replica, will help you visualize and understand the system.

Scientists create representational models of all sorts of things ranging from cells to oceans, and as they get more sophisticated, they become less visually representative and more numerically and computer based. For example, if we were to take a field trip to NOAA's weather headquarters, all we would see is a room filled with huge computers that would be modeling possible weather outcomes given the current conditions. The models in this case are not visual: they are mathematical algorithms. We use mathematical models in our classrooms as well when we plot plant growth over time or represent class height on a bar graph.

There are many ways to model your favorite system, and for K–5 students, effective models may be visual or three-dimensional such as dioramas, figures, Lego worlds, cutaways, and flowcharts. In the following chart, we share some ideas for familiar models you might use in your classroom.

Examples of System Models

Model	Possible interacting components	System represented by model
Monopoly	Players, property, bank, money	Real estate and banking systems
Mobile of the solar system	Planets and Sun	Solar system
Map of your city or town	Roads, rivers, bridges, mountains, parks, neighborhoods	Your city or town
Diagram or cutaway of digestive system	Mouth, throat, stomach, intestines	Digestive system
Poster with flowchart showing "Where does our food come from?"	Farmers, transportation, stores, eaters	Food system

In addition to helping us understand complex systems in the natural world, models can also be used to solve problems in the engineered world that are impractical, enormous (think scale), or unsafe. What's the best way to get to school? At the beginning of the school year, bus drivers do not drive around trying to determine the best routes; their routes have already been modeled and they know where to go. How much and what kind of steel will the new San Francisco–Oakland Bay Bridge need? A model such as a computer simulation will answer these questions. How many planes can land at the airport per hour? We wouldn't sign up for that experiment, but a model would get us the answer safely.

What If Questions

Models clearly help us conceptualize and understand systems, but their true beauty is that they allow us to ask *what if* on a safe stage. Our dentist recently considered planting a larger terrarium in a sunnier window, and asked Mark, her favorite plant biologist, whether it would grow well there. Moved to the sunnier window, her smaller terrarium could be used as a model to answer her *what if* question. *What if* questions are a way of asking how a change might affect the system, and models allow us to test different possible outcomes. Picture a heart model and ask, "What if I removed this valve? Or constricted this artery?" These are the types of questions that help people understand heart disease. Whether it be in engineering or in the natural world, done correctly, models allow us us to answer *what if* questions with a strong degree of certainty when it is difficult or impossible (or unwise) to get the answer any other way.

In science, *what if* questions fall into three categories. The first category considers what happens inside the system. What if the interactions change between the components? A question like this allows you to explore the cause-and-effect relationships within the system. You might ask, "What if I changed the seating in my classroom, would it affect student interactions?" Similarly, we could ask, "What if we moved the plants within the terrarium, what effect would this have on this tiny ecosystem?"

Next, scientists ask, "What if the matter or energy entering and leaving the system changes?" In open systems, energy and matter flow in and out of the system; a dog eats food, energy is captured, and waste comes out. These two inputs—*energy and matter*—form a crosscutting concept themselves and are the primary agents of change in systems. When energy is added to the terrarium as light, the system changes because the plants photosynthesize and grow, which triggers a cascade of other events. We could ask, "What if I moved the terrarium to a sunnier window? What would be the effect on the components?"

Finally, the third question asks, "What if the external forces acting on the system change?" External forces like gravity often play a role in models of the natural world, but are absolutely critical in engineering models. Bridges are load-bearing structures and the force of the load is determined by the gravitational pull and the weight of the object. An engineer might ask, "What if three eighteen-wheelers cross this bridge at the same time?" In the following, we share our thinking on how to use *what if* questions.

Because a model is a representation of a system, it is always wise to ask, "How accurate is the model?" Much of science is about developing, testing, and refining models for accuracy. We know an accurate model when we see one because its predictions are reliable. Did the 3-D model in your state park get you to the scenic overlook as planned or did it turn your one-hour walk into half a day? If you got lost, perhaps this working model should be updated.

How we use models in the natural and engineered world

Types of model	Use model to:		
	Show how the system works	Ask *what if* questions	Predict outcomes of *what if* questions
Monopoly (engineered world)	Represents an economic system	What if Ila owns all of the property?	All the other players will go bankrupt. Because this is an economic model, we can predict what will happen if we concentrate wealth in our economy.
Weather model (natural world)	Represents and helps us communicate the patterns and cause-and-effect relationships in the atmosphere	What if the front stalls above the city?	If the front stalls, the rain will continue into the afternoon.
A 3-D scaled map of a state park (engineered world)	Represents the park's features and communicates where to hike, picnic, and swim	What if we took a different trail to the overlook?	It would be faster but less scenic.
Model of a proposed bridge (engineered world)	Represents bridge designed to span a local stream	What if a school bus and a large truck cross at the same time?	The model will reveal whether two large vehicles can cross simultaneously.

Energy and Matter Are the Movers and Shakers of Systems

As we will explain in the next chapter, energy and matter affect systems and we can see this play out in first-grade teacher Rebecca's aquarium. It has all the expected components: fish, plants, a bubbler, a heater, a castle, and a light, but it's the interactions between them that are the good stuff. There are many cause-and-effect relationships in the system, and they are all driven by the matter and energy that flow through it. In an aquarium like Rebecca's, fish swim, sleep, fight, mate, eat their young, and hide in the castle. Matter can flow into the system and that is exactly what happens when Rebecca's students feed the fish. The fish food (matter) that is added from the outside is converted to energy. The heater adds energy that flows into the system and warms the water, and the bubbler adds oxygen (matter) to the system. This is why we love aquariums: the components, the interactions, the boundary, and the flow of energy and matter constitute a visible ecosystem.

Rebecca's aquarium is a system but we can also use it as a model to understand certain processes in a larger aquatic system like a pond. First grader Vernon recognized that an aquarium is also a model when he described it as "a man-made ocean." When Rebecca asked her class to pose *what if* questions, the students came up with several interesting ones. The children asked, "What if the filter stopped? The water got hotter? We removed the plants? Added more fish?" Notice that their spontaneous questions all involve energy and matter, the primary instigator of change in systems. Rebecca created a lesson where her students were invited to observe a system, "Bob's tank," that was then used to model what would happen in a similar system on a much larger scale such as a real pond. Notice how Emma uses Bob's tank to model what would happen if the water temperature rose (a change in energy) in a real pond (see Figure 6.2).

You have probably noticed that systems are filled with patterns; we already know what the fish are up to in the aquarium. The aquarium's components are patterns and their interactions are patterns. To think like a scientist is to engage the superpowers of pattern and apply them to the system. When Rebecca's class notes that the aquarium is cloudy, they can summon the superpowers and use their background knowledge to apply them to the problem.

- *Classifying*: How do we know a healthy aquarium when we see one? When the water is clear and doesn't smell. If we know the patterns that define the system, we can classify the aquarium as healthy or not.

- *Questioning* (cause and effect): What if we adjust the bubbler? What effect will this have on the system? Will it clear up the cloudiness and smell?

- *Predicting*: If we know the system's patterns, we can predict the effects of *what if* questions. The bubbler (cause) will clear up the cloudiness (effect) because the microbes will be able to do their work better (mechanism).

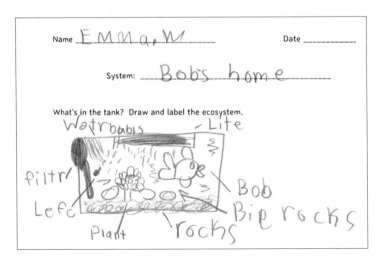

Figure 6.2
Emma's drawing shows that Bob's tank has interacting components.

Developing Habits of Mind About Systems and System Models

How do you know a system when you see one? The key is to identify the pattern (the boundaries and the interacting components) that defines the system. What you see or measure in a system are the effects produced by cause-and-effect relationships. A model represents a system and allows you to ask *what if*. Use the following questions to help you identify and understand any system and work with a model.

- To identify the boundary of a system, ask: "Where does it begin and where does it end?" Remember the boundary can be physical, mathematical, or social like a team, herd, or clique.

- To identify the components and how they are interacting, ask: "What are the parts of the system and what are they doing?"

- Ask: "What if?" A model is a representation of a system and allows us to ask *what if* questions. Questions like these allow us to use models to safely predict outcomes in a system. This is particularly important in the application of science and engineering.

Is It Love or Is It Chemistry?

Have you ever noticed that each of your classes has its own personality? Even more intriguing is that the group behavior is not always predictable no matter how carefully we orchestrate class placements. Systems have what scientists call *emergent properties*. These are effects that cannot be predicted even if we know the behaviors of the components in advance. It is a property that emerges from the system itself. For example, humans are made primarily of six elements: carbon, hydrogen, oxygen, nitrogen, sulfur, and phosphorous. We know a lot about these elements and how they react. Can we use this understanding to predict how a system (the human) will function or behave? Not really. Even understanding these six elements wouldn't allow us to predict that seven-year-old Lars likes to skip at recess. Life itself is an emergent property because the behaviors and characteristics of organisms cannot be predicted from their interacting components, which means love really is more than chemistry.

Exploring Systems and System Models in Children's Literature

Books invite us to visit a *system*—it's the whole point of the book. We get to visit an alternate system, so no matter the genre or topic, we can always explore our key ideas: the characters and settings are the *interacting components* and *boundaries*, and through the text we learn *what happens, why, and how*, as well as how the *outside influences* affect the system. Because books themselves are representations—there is no actual hurricane in the book—they model places, events, patterns, and systems. They allow us to experience aspects of life vicariously and understand *what* would happen *if*. Author Katherine Paterson was once asked whether a child who had lost a friend should read *Bridge to Terabithia* because it addresses this same tragedy. Paterson replied that it may be too late—children benefit from reading about loss and other life passages before they experience them firsthand. This is the power of books as models; they allow us to experience and visit social or scientific systems, which deepens our understanding of society, science, and the world.

Books That Shout Systems and System Models

Many types of nonfiction, particularly survey books, *shout* systems and explore models scientifically, explaining how the components interact and respond to external influences like matter and energy. Books about animals, plants, and ecosystems will usually feature interacting components within a specified boundary. Often authors will present subsystems to help the reader understand the whole system. For example *Up in the Garden and Down in the Dirt* (Messner) helps us understand how a garden works by focusing our attention on one of the important subsystems, the soil. Through stylized cutaways, we see the components of a garden and how they interact. Energy and matter in the form of sun and rain influence the interactions of the garden components.

Nonfiction is where models really shine. Authors decide the best ways to represent components and interactions, and this is where thumbnail illustrations, close-ups, diagrams, cutaways, cross sections, and timelines serve as models of real phenomena. A cross section allows us to ask, "What if we could see inside?" This is exactly what Gail Gibbons does in *Planet Earth/ Inside Out* to show us what the earth's core looks like. Similarly, because we can't encapsulate a real hurricane in a book, authors use well-designed models to help us answer our *what if* questions. What if a hurricane hits the east coast of Florida? A timeline and map may show the formation and intensity of a particular hurricane. The use of models extends beyond children's literature, and we encounter them in digital and printed media regularly. Websites like National Geographic Kids offer *interactive* models that are often presented as games to help students understand systems such as frogs and ears.

A book like *When the Wolves Returned* (Patent) describes how the reintroduction of wolves dramatically improved the ecosystem of Yellowstone National Park. If you share a book like this with your students, you might start by examining the system described. Because this book is about the transformation of Yellowstone's ecosystem, focus on the wolf's role. The wolf, a critical component, was hunted to local extinction, which changed how the other components interacted. The herbivores, freed from the threat of the wolf, overgrazed the plants and this disrupted cycles in the ecosystem. Reintroducing the wolf restored the system to its original equilibrium. This is a great success story, but the power of a book like this is to ask what we learned about the system and how we can apply it to other systems. In this case, knowing how wolves affected Yellowstone's ecosystem enables us to ask, "What if we brought the wolf (or mountain lion) back to our state? What can we learn and predict using Yellowstone as a model?"

Book Selection and Beginning Conversations

First, find your boundaries. In a good systems book, the boundaries are clear. In some ways you want a book that is like Rebecca's aquarium where the glass edge is an easily recognizable boundary. In an analogous way, look for books where the boundaries of the world or topic the author has written about are easily recognized. You might look for books that feature:

• A well-recognized physical boundary such as an animal, zoo, island, or dollhouse. The strength of these systems is that the boundary is tangible and defines the system for you; it's everything within the space created by the boundary.

• A process in the natural or engineered world (think function or behavior) such as making honey or digestion. In this type of book, authors often examine the system by focusing on the subsystems; a book on digestion may feature the mouth, stomach, and intestines and a book on honey may include bees, flowers, and nectar.

Following, we offer ideas for how you might discuss systems using books. No matter the system or genre, these questions will help you identify the boundaries and interacting components and explore *what if* in any type of book. Get started here with shout books, and revisit the table when you're reading a whisper book.

In Figure 6.3 you'll find a beginning list of books for exploring systems and system models. Those of you familiar with these titles might notice a pattern—all but two of these books (*Jack's Garden* and *Winter Barn*) are nonfiction. As our list suggests, when choosing shout books, you will have more success with nonfiction.

NONFICTION	NONFICTION
One Small Place in a Tree (Brenner)	*Up in the Garden and Down in the Dirt* (Messner)
Before We Eat: From Farm to Table (Brisson)	*Crashed, Smashed, and Mashed: A Trip to Junkyard Heaven* (Mitchell)
Jack's Garden (Cole)	*Every Last Drop* (Mulder)
Green City: How One Community Survived a Tornado and Rebuilt for a Sustainable Future (Drummond)	*When the Wolves Returned* (Patent)
The Wolves Are Back (George)	*Winter Barn* (Parnall)
Emergency! (Gibbons)	*One Plastic Bag* (Paul)
Zoo (Gibbons)	*Our Community Garden* (Pollak)
In the Garden with Dr. Carver (Grigsby)	*My Librarian Is a Camel* (Ruurs)
Oil Spill! Disaster in the Gulf of Mexico (Landau)	*The Busy Tree* (Ward)

Figure 6.3

A beginning list of books that shout systems and system models

Mentor Texts Are Models for Writing Nonfiction

Ralph Fletcher says that we can only write as well as we read because effective writing in any genre requires good models. Many of us know these models as mentor texts. When we read excellent writing, we can learn to be better communicators if we pay attention to what the model can teach us. When your students are writing about systems such as ecosystems, community services, or the body, lean on books by mentor authors like Gibbons, Jenkins, and Sayre. Books by these authors consistently model how to communicate complex systems effectively using narrative and illustrations that function as visual models. Because models allow us to ask "What if?" you might encourage your students to ask questions like, "What if Steve Jenkins or Gail Gibbons were writing about this? Would they use a scale diagram or a thumbnail illustration?"

TALK PROMPTS for exploring systems and system models in books that shout

Examples of genre	Synopsis of sample book	Ask: "Where does the system begin and end? What are the components?"	Ask: "What is happening in the system and why (cause and effect)?"	Ask: "What are the outside influences on the system? And what is the effect?"	Ask: "What if . . . ?"
The Honey makers (Gibbons) Nonfiction survey book	Gibbons uses diagrams, close-ups, and labels to model the process of making honey.	A meadow or even your neighborhood forms the boundaries for the system that is honey production. The components are bees, hive, flowers, and beekeepers.	The interactions are: bees collect nectar, waggle, pollinate flowers, and make honey. Beekeepers manage the hives.	Weather and sun influence the bees and plants, and bears disrupt the hive when they steal honey.	What if no flowers bloomed? What if we had six weeks of rain? What would be the effect on the honey?

Gail Gibbons' Middle Name Should Be *System*

We perused 100+ titles from Gail Gibbons and found that the majority of them are about a specific system. After reading *Tell Me, Tree* for the first time, Mark closed the book and confided to Valerie, "Wow, that's my entire plant biology college course in a much more accessible format." Pick up any of Gibbons' books and you are likely to find a system and its subsystems presented through text, cutaways, diagrams, and cross sections. For example, in *The Honey Makers* we see a cross section (a model) of a flower on one page, a bee on another, and a diagram of a beehive (another model) on a third page. Each of these is a system in itself and is a component in the larger system of honey production; taken together they form the boundary. By presenting the honey-making process as a series of steps made up of subsystems, Gibbons does exactly what scientists often do to help us understand a system—she divides it into a series of smaller interacting systems.

Topic Spotlight: Gardens

School gardens are a rich topic for cultivating an understanding of systems. While visiting a school, we heard students talking about raised beds, plants, and even the soil; it would be easy to help students identify these as systems. Their discussion inspired us to grab *Compost Stew* (Siddals) off our shelf, and we noticed that every page was filled with systems like wheelbarrows, farm animals, and pumpkins. Like scientists, we started by defining the boundaries of the system we wanted to discuss—the compost bin. When using a book like this we might ask, "How do you know where the compost bin begins and ends?" On one page we see the answer: a black barrel forms the physical boundary of this system. The rest of the book features children adding bananas, eggshells, grass clippings, and other organic matter to the pile. These illustrations provide an opportunity to ask, "What's in the compost?" These are the interacting components, along with bacteria, worms, and all the things that turn the matter into compost. What are they doing? Rotting. We might even ask a *what if* question like "What if we put a plastic jug in the compost? Would it rot?" Although we focused on a compost bin as a system, you can use any of the systems in a garden or even the whole garden itself for your exploration of systems. Remember that you can also use gardens as a model and ask *what if* questions like, "What if our new peach tree thrives here? Where else can we plant it in the state?"

Books That Whisper Systems and System Models

Whisper books are outside of the realm of science and often feature relationship-based systems such as stories about classrooms, families, and friends. These books clearly describe a system, but we call them whisper books because the key ideas apply to social rather than scientific systems. They whisper about the key ideas in systems and system models, so we might see them as a literary stepping-stone to reading like a scientist.

In fiction, authors use interacting components to create a story, and we might think of a plot as the interactions of the system created by the author. When authors describe the setting, they are letting us know the boundaries of their story's system. The characters are the components acting inside that system, and the story itself—the plot—is the author's exploration of *what if* questions. The three ways we might apply *what if* questions in science also create predictable plotlines in fiction. There might be changes in the interactions *within* the system (best friends argue), or changes in the flow of matter and energy *across* the system (the class has a substitute teacher). Because we are talking about fiction, the author doesn't have to abide by the rules of the natural world; the story system might be influenced by a force like a wizard's invisibility cloak, time travel, or a magic pasta pot.

For example, *Amber on the Mountain* (Johnston) tells the story of a remote Rocky Mountain town that cannot recruit a teacher to start a local school. When Anna, the daughter of a road surveyor, spends a few months in the town, she teaches Amber how to read. We might view this book as the story of a closed system (the remote village) whose interacting components change when an outside influence (the road) brings new energy and matter to town. We can even go one step further and call this book a model for rural small town life. What if we built a road in our town? What would be the effect on our school, daily life, and relationships? Books as models help readers understand social systems such as cultures, government, or religion.

Often in fiction, the interactions between the components are complex and include emotions in addition to the rules of the natural world. For example, a landslide is caused by the rules of the natural world, but it also evokes an emotional response that may propel a character to snatch another out of harm's way. Friends fight, parents worry, a lost dog is found. We can actually swap familiar literary terms like *characters* and *settings* for *components* and *boundaries*, and *plot* for *interactions* caused by internal and external influences. The similarity in these literary and scientific terms may help many young fiction mavens make a seamless transition to reading like a scientist. (See Figure 6.4 for a beginning list of books that whisper social or scientific systems or system models.)

TALK PROMPTS to help you code switch between literary and scientific terms

Story elements in *Cinderella*	Using the literary language of fiction, call this element . . .	Using the scientific language of systems, call this element . . .
Cottage, castle, pumpkin carriage	Setting	Boundary
Cinderella, stepmother, stepsisters, fairy godmother, prince	Characters	Components
• Adjusting to new family • Death of Cinderella's father • Preferential treatment to some family members • Magic • Romance with Prince • Right shoe size	Events that shape character development and plot points	Interacting components influenced by energy and matter

FICTION

Wanda's Roses (Brisson)

Fly Away Home (Bunting)

One Green Apple (Bunting)

The Little House (Burton)

Diary of a Worm (Cronin)

My Map Book (Fanelli)

In the Tall, Tall Grass (Fleming), younger readers

In the Small, Small Pond (Fleming), younger readers

The Wild Boy (Gerstein)

Chrysanthemum (Henkes)

Julius, the Baby of the World (Henkes)

The Hello, Goodbye Window (Juster)

Roxaboxen (McLerran)

Last Stop on Market Street (Peña)

Farmer Duck (Waddell)

Figure 6.4

A beginning list of books that whisper social or scientific systems or system models

Science Fiction and Fantasy Are Based on *What If*

Science fiction and fantasy worlds deserve special attention because their entire premise is based on *what if*. The system—whether Middle Earth, Narnia, or Hogwarts—is successful when it is internally consistent. If the author is skilled, we know how the components will interact because they follow the rules established in the narrative. If you are attacked by a Dementor, eat some chocolate. A medieval fantasy world that is suddenly attacked by a spaceship is sure to lose its readers. In fantasy, the *what if* reveals the author's imagination. On the other hand, many science fiction writers are scientists or have science advisors who help them create futuristic worlds that play *what if* with emerging technologies. The popular *Jurassic Park* books are an example of how Michael Crichton asks, "What if we used genetic technologies to bring dinosaurs back to life?"

The first three concepts (pattern, cause and effect, and structure and function) established the foundation for thinking like a scientist. The next step is to start to see these three concepts in systems. How do we know a system when we see one? Each system has a defining pattern: its boundary and interacting components. When we see a white box with bees flying in and out, we know this is a beehive because we recognize the boundary and interacting components. The interacting components within the system—the bees, the honey, and the combs—are involved in cause-and-effect relationships, and as we will see in the next chapter they are fueled by energy and matter as the bees bring nectar and pollen to the hive.

7

ENERGY AND MATTER

Let's Get the Ball Rolling

Learning and Teaching the Science

What You Need to Know: *Four Ways to Think About Energy and Matter*

On our way to a third-grade classroom, we noticed two girls thumb wrestling, another one eating yogurt, and a pair of boys walking down the hall toward their classroom. Outside, two students were raising the flag while a late parent sprinted toward the building with a school-age child in tow and a screaming three-year-old trailing in the distance. This endearing scene happens daily at just about every school and perfectly captures the role of energy and matter in our lives. (See Figure 7.1.)

We are all familiar with matter and energy on this human scale. We are made of matter, walk on matter, breathe matter, and even eat matter. Energy is the fuel that makes things happen. Energy is the fuel that powers the flag raisers and the thumb wrestlers. The goal for elementary students is to develop a familiarity with how matter and energy work in the

Figure 7.1
The foot above the dollhouse implies that something ominous is about to happen to this system. Olivia shows her understanding that *energy and matter* are the two primary influences that cause things to happen.

world and are involved in literally everything they do. To reach this goal, there are four key ideas students will need to understand.

The World Is Made of Matter

When working with children, we like to start by helping them understand matter because it is all around us, often visible, and typically we can touch it. Ask your students to look around the classroom and notice objects. These are all made of matter. The pencils, scissors, desks, water in the sink, and the floor are made of matter. When we visited a third-grade class, Susannah shared with us how to spot matter by explaining, "It is made of stuff." We like this working definition because it is a clear way of saying *matter is made of particles* (such as atoms) that we can recognize as solids, liquids, or gases. When we asked if air is matter, Eliot hit it right on the nose when he said, "Air is made of stuff, too, like oxygen."

Recognizing that stuff is matter is an important first step and your next step is to help students realize that matter cannot go away nor can it magically appear. This is why second grader Daphne was dubious while watching a magician pull a rabbit out of her hat. "That's a trick, because you can't just make something appear." She also knew that the assistant did not really disappear. Daphne recognized these tricks for what they are—a clever ruse—because even at a young age most children have already learned that you can't make something out of nothing or make things magically disappear. Daphne's observations perfectly describe one of the key ideas of matter: it doesn't go away and it doesn't magically appear.

Matter Can Transform

Matter may not appear or disappear, but it can transform. Your students have already noticed this characteristic in fantasy and science fiction. Werewolves transform from human to wolf, and Clark Kent becomes Superman. A birthday cake is a more realistic example. To make a cake, you have to transform matter—eggs, flour, sugar, and chocolate—into a cake using energy. When the cake comes out of the oven all of the stuff, the matter, is still there but it has been transformed into a delightful treat that you can eat without any fear of *Salmonella*.

Matter transforms around us all the time. Sometimes the transformation is reversible like an ice cube melting into water and then refreezing into ice. Other times it is irreversible like the baked cake—you can't retrieve the eggs no matter how hard you might try because they have been irreversibly transformed. Because matter doesn't go away, have you ever wondered what happens to the cake after you eat it? Where does it go and what does it turn into? You know it doesn't go away because the laws of physics do not allow that possibility. Believe it or not, most of the cake is transformed into carbon dioxide, which you exhale. Only a surprisingly small part of it eventually gets flushed down the toilet. Once lit, the candles on the birthday cake are also transformed and third grader Raj got it right when he figured out that "the flame turns the candles into a gas."

Energy Takes Many Forms

If we think of matter as "stuff," then we can think of energy as the fuel for making matter dance. We're all familiar with energy as it relates to our bodies or conservation efforts in many of our schools, but energy is much more than this. Energy is everywhere and appears in many forms such as motion, light, heat, sound, electricity, and chemical reactions (think food). When we experience energy as motion, light, heat, or sound, these are all forms of *kinetic* energy—something is moving. When we hear the bell ring, the sound moving into our ears is a form of kinetic energy. When we touch the warm radiator, the heat flowing into our hands is a form of kinetic energy. When the pencil is rolling across the classroom floor, this kinetic energy takes the form of motion. When we turn on the light after quiet time, the light illuminating the room is actually kinetic energy coming into our eyes. Energy may not be made of stuff but it is all around us, fueling everything that happens. Just remember, if there is motion, heat, light, or sound, there is kinetic energy.

Energy can also be stored, meaning it is there but it's at rest. We call stored energy *potential energy,* and a loose parallel is when we ruefully observe that a capable student has yet to complete an assignment. With the word *yet*, we are referring to that student's potential: she could do it, but just hasn't. Potential energy is similar. Something could happen, it just hasn't happened yet. To unleash potential energy and convert it to kinetic energy, we have to add *activation energy*. Activation energy is similar to the motivation you might provide your student with an encouraging comment.

There's nothing like a ball and a slide to explain potential, kinetic, and activation energy. Place a ball on the flat top of a slide. Nothing is happening to the ball. It is at rest but we know something *could* happen. In this state the ball has potential energy because it *could* roll down the slide if nudged. The energy is stored but it has not been released. Transfer some energy to the ball by giving it a little push. The push is the activation energy that will release the potential energy stored in the ball. Even your intention to push the ball is fueled by energy in your brain. As the ball rolls down the slide, it is in motion, which is kinetic energy. Because we know that energy can't magically appear, where did the potential energy in the ball come from? The source of the potential energy is you! You used energy to carry the ball up the ladder, and part of this energy was transferred to the ball when you placed it at a greater height—it can now go into motion down the slide.

We all know that when a student skips breakfast before school, it may be a rough day. Realizing the importance of getting some energy into kids before school, many districts provide breakfast. Food is potential energy stored in the molecules that make up our eggs, hot sauce, and croissants. The energy stored in our food is called *chemical energy*. Chemical energy can be kinetic energy like a fire or potential energy like a chocolate bar. When we digest our food, the energy stored in it flows into our bodies, which then leaves as motion, sound, and heat when we walk, talk, and maintain our body temperature. Because energy never goes away, where did the stored energy in our breakfast cereal come from? It came from the sun. Plants harvest light energy, which they store as chemical energy, and this energy flows through people and animals when they eat plants or when we eat animals that eat plants. To think like a scientist is to realize that *food* is synonymous with *potential energy*.

Energy Provides the Fuel for Things to Happen

Energy, like matter, does not go away or magically appear, but rather it flows into and out of matter and systems fueling change. It's sort of like the game "Pass the Energy," which you might know as "Pass the Squeeze." In this game, students hold hands in a circle and a squeeze (the energy) is passed in one direction around the circle one squeeze at a time. When Donna squeezes Mac's hand, she has symbolically transferred energy and now Mac is free to squeeze Denise's hand, which transfers the energy again. Staying frozen in between squeezes will help students realize that without energy, nothing can happen.

All your students who have played a sport involving balls have experienced energy transfer. Every time your students kick, bat, catch, block, or throw a ball, energy is being transferred to and from the ball. Energy is the fuel that makes things happen. How does energy fuel things? It *acts on* matter by being transferred. Kick a ball and what happens? The motion of your foot transfers energy to the ball (see Figure 7.2). We can even hear and see the energy that the ball has accepted from your foot in two forms: a satisfying thump sound and the ball in motion. In the classroom, we can hear the bell ring because energy as sound transfers to and then acts on our eardrums. We can feel the radiator heat because the energy transfers to our hand just like the light energy transfers to our eyes after we flip on the light switch. When Pico moves his hand, energy transfers to the pencil putting it in motion. The key is to remember that matter accepts the transfer of energy by making a sound, heating up, giving off light, or going into motion.

We actually refer to energy transfer every time we use a verb that ends in -*ing*. Words that tell us something is happening like *kicking, reading, eating*, and *driving* also tell us that energy is being transferred. Energy does not go away (this is one of the golden rules of science), it transfers or flows through matter and systems and by doing so provides the fuel for cause-and-effect relationships as presented in the table on the following page.

Energy causes things to happen and the amount of energy is also important. Remember the Goldilocks scale? The right amount is relative and this is also true for energy. Too much energy

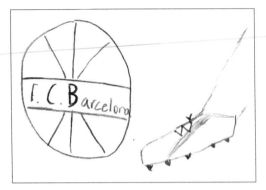

Figure 7.2

Energy in the form of a foot in motion is about transfer to the soccer ball.

transferred from Geoffrey's foot to the soccer ball may cause the ball to soar over the goal. Too little energy and Mila, the goalie, can easily grab the ball. Think of your kitchen and the last time you were making hot chocolate from scratch. If you added too much energy, your beverage probably burned. We actually monitor our body's energy use all the time and this is apparent in the language we use. "I'm hungry" is our way of saying "I need energy. I am tired means my fuel is running low." "Hurry up" or "Speak louder" says "Put more energy into the system." When we say "I need to lose weight," we're really saying "I need to get rid of some potential energy."

Energy forms and transfer of energy

Energy form	What did the energy fuel?	Energy transfer
Motion	Swinging bat that hits the home run	Batter to bat to ball
Heat	Mug of cocoa	Stove element to pot to cocoa
Sound	Singing	Vocal chords to air to eardrums
Light	Production of electricity	Sunlight to solar panel to electricity
Food	Libby jumping rope	Oatmeal to Libby's muscles eventually (through chemical reactions)

Developing Your Lens: Energy In, Energy Out—The Big Idea for Getting Friendly with Energy

Scientists like to use the phrase *energy in, energy out*, which is a shortcut for saying that energy doesn't go away; it flows by transferring in its different forms to and from matter and while transferring, it causes something to happen. To think like a scientist is to remember that if something is happening, energy is at play in the system. We can see energy in, energy out every day in our classroom. When we turn on the lights in the morning, electric energy flows into the lightbulb as motion, something happens in the bulb, and then this energy leaves as light and heat. Similarly, when our students blow into a recorder, energy flows into the instrument, causing it to vibrate, and then this energy flows out of the recorder as sound.

I'll Have a Double Scoop of Energy on a Sugar Cone, Please

We often joke that Ben and Jerry created a successful ice cream company because their flavors speak to our energy cravings. Eating is our favorite way of personally exploring energy transfer. That is, after all, why we eat—to transfer the potential energy in the food into our body. Tasty food like ice cream is energy dense; that is why we think it is tasty. The tongue is actually a fine-tuned sensor that detects energy that tastes sweet or fatty. If you list your students' favorite foods, we bet what they would have in common is that they are high in energy, in other words, calories. Your students love these foods because humans evolved a taste system housed in the tongue that detects energy and our brain rewards us with pleasure when we gobble down a high-energy food like peanut butter ice cream with chocolate chunks.

When working with students, it's easiest to start by identifying the energy that flows out of matter because typically this is something that we can see or measure. Consider using this line of thinking:

- Start by picking a system. Remember, as a scientist you delineate the boundaries, but a good starting place is to pick a person, animal, or machine as your system.

- Ask: "What is the system (bike, bird, student)?"

- To reveal what the system is doing, ask: "Is the system moving, making a sound, giving off light or heat?" If it is doing any of these then energy is flowing through it, causing these effects.

The bottom line is, when we see a bird flying, hear Elsa singing, or see a school bus rumbling by our classroom, we know energy is flowing through each of these systems because they are doing something. Of course, at any given time, a system may not be doing anything, like a bike that is leaning against a wall. This system is at rest because no energy is flowing through it (but it may still have potential energy).

Matter accepts and transfers energy and sometimes when energy flows through matter it is transformed. This is what happens when we bake cookies or cook scrambled eggs. Other times, matter is not transformed when energy flows through it. When we hear the crack of a bat striking a baseball, a sound is made and the ball goes into motion but neither the ball nor the bat is transformed. To help your students develop a lens for seeing how the transfer of energy can fuel transformation, ask, "Is the system the same after the energy flowed through it?" In the case of the ball it is, but cookies are very different beasts after they leave the oven.

QUICK START QUESTIONS TO
Spot the Energy Flow and Matter Transformation in Systems

Identify the system	To reveal energy in, ask: "What is the fuel: motion, heat, sound, food, light, or electricity?"	To reveal energy out, ask: "What is the (system) doing?" Look for heat, sound, light, motion, electricity, or photosynthesis if the system is a plant.	To spot matter transformation, ask: "Is the (system) the same after the energy flowed through it?"
Clarinet	The *motion* from Chad's breath causes the clarinet to vibrate.	It is making *sound*.	Is the clarinet the same? Yes. Chad's breath did not melt the clarinet.
Bike	The fuel is the *motion* of Reiko's legs.	It is *moving* because Reiko is riding it down the street.	Is the bike the same? Yes. The bike is not transformed by riding it (unless Reiko crashes).
Campfire	Wood is the fuel, which was formed with *light* energy from the sun.	The fire is bright and hot because it is burning.	Is the campfire the same? No. The wood is transformed into a gas. The wood is not wood anymore.
Boiling water	The fuel is *heat* from the burner.	The boiling water is *hot* and giving off *heat*.	Is the water the same? Yes. The water is still water even though it has changed states.
Soccer ball	The *motion* from Asher's leg caused the ball to soar.	The soccer ball is sailing toward the far post.	Is the ball the same? Yes. After being kicked, all of us still recognize it as a soccer ball.
Dog	The dog eats food.	The dog is barking, running, and fetching.	Is the dog the same? Yes. The dog is the same after it plays.

Exploring Energy and Matter in Children's Literature

Children's book characters ride bikes, carry pigs up hills, and eat their way through fruit, cupcakes, and ice cream to build a cocoon. Little engines find that they can make it up the mountain, and wizards transform herbs into potions. You will find that your library is already filled with books that shout *energy in, energy out* or *matter transforms*. Just about any book that explores photosynthesis or how an organism grows is a good bet for energy in, energy out in the natural world. Books involving sports or transportation are going to scream energy transfer in the engineered world. Water is a rich topic for examining how matter transforms—think ice, water, and steam. In whisper books, if you can answer the questions "What's happening?" and "What's fueling it?," you can spot the energy transfer. Humpty Dumpty is the perfect, albeit tragic, example of energy transfer. The energy in motion of Humpty's fall is transferred to his shell at the moment of his abrupt stop. This energy transfer can be heard and seen in the horrid crack. We also know that this is an irreversible transformation of matter. Not even all the King's horses and men could put him together again.

Books That Shout Energy and Matter

You have probably noticed that energy transfer is kind of like cause and effect: if something is happening, energy is involved. Every book offers us a chance to see energy out because the system—whether a person, machine, or the weather—is doing something. Shout books explore types, forms, and transfers of energy, and you will recognize a book that shouts because its text and illustrations show readers the mechanisms of how energy flows in and out of systems. Most of these are nonfiction. In a book like *It's Raining!* by Gail Gibbons, we come to understand the role that energy from the sun plays in cycling water. We see this when the sun evaporates ocean water, which falls as rain that eventually joins a river. This approach of showing how energy fuels something is what defines a shout book.

Book Selection and Beginning Conversations

Many appealing and accurate series books published by National Geographic, Smithsonian, and NSTA Kids (among others) shout energy in the context of systems. You may notice these books feature many examples of types, forms, and transfers of energy, so start by picking a single page or two during a read-aloud, and summon the quick start questions to engage your students. Here's how you might do this with a page in a book about the natural world, and one about the engineered world.

TALK PROMPTS for exploring the energy flow and matter transformation in shout books

Identify the system.	To reveal energy in, ask: "What is the fuel?"	To reveal energy out, ask: "What is the (system) doing?" Look for heat, sound, light, motion, electricity, or photosynthesis if the system is a plant.	To spot *matter transformation*, ask: "Is the (system) the same after the energy flowed through it?"
Energy and matter in the natural world **A close look at one page in *Why Do Elephants Need the Sun?* (Wells)**			
We see a food web (the system) that begins with plants and ends with elephants.	The fuel is the sun, which provides light energy for the plants to harvest through photosynthesis.	The animals are going about the motions of their daily lives such as eating and walking. The plants are photosynthesizing.	As shown in the illustration, matter is transformed in this food web. Plants convert carbon dioxide into plant matter as they grow. The monkeys and elephants eat the plants and breathe out carbon dioxide.
Energy and matter in the engineered world **A close look at one page in *The Shocking Truth About Energy* (Leedy)**			
On a double-page spread we see a wind turbine as the system.	The fuel for the turbine is the wind.	The turbine is moving as the wind blows across it, which generates electricity.	There is no transformation of matter. The turbine is the same after the wind blows across it.

Shout books like the ones in Figure 7.3 can help you explore matter and energy with your class. As we illustrated in the table above, start by identifying the system and then ask: "What is it doing? What's fueling it? Is this system the same after the energy flowed through it?"

Topic Spotlight: Earth—A Complex System with a High-Energy Friend

Earth is the ultimate system for humans and like all systems, energy flows through it. Where does the energy that flows into Earth's system come from? The answer is almost always the sun. Plants harvest light energy (think photosynthesis) and store this energy, which animals transfer to their bodies when they eat the plants. Your breakfast is really just a big spoonful of sunshine. Even the eggs, milk, and bacon come from the sun because chickens, cows, and pigs also eat plants. The sun powers so much more than our food. Picture a meandering river. The water is in motion so there must be energy involved, but where did it come from? The sun. The sun caused water to evaporate, which then fell as rain that flowed into the river. The sun is even responsible for the wind because wind is created by the sun's heat.

Buried Sunlight (Bang and Chisolm)	*The Boy Who Harnessed the Wind* (Kamkwamba and Mealer)
Living Sunlight (Bang and Chisolm)	*The Shocking Truth About Energy* (Leedy)
My Light (Bang)	*All the Water in the World* (Lyon)
Ocean Sunlight (Bang and Chisolm)	*Crashed, Smashed, and Mashed* (Mitchell)
Energy Island (Drummond)	*Water Is Water* (Paul)
Hurricanes! (Gibbons)	*Stars Beneath Your Bed* (Sayre)
It's Raining! (Gibbons)	*Trout Are Made of Trees* (Sayre)
Tell Me, Tree (Gibbons)	*Compost Stew* (Siddals)
Tornadoes! (Gibbons)	*What Happens to a Hamburger?* (Showers)

Figure 7.3

A beginning list of books that shout energy and matter

Molly Bang and Penny Chisolm have a quartet of brilliant picture books that explain how the sun powers systems in both the natural and engineered world. In their book, *Living Sunlight: How Plants Bring the Earth to Life*, they describe how plants harvest light energy, which they store as chemical energy. This chemical energy flows through deer, rabbits, humans, and anything else that eats plants. In their other books, *My Light* and *Buried Sunlight*, we learn that

Molly Bang's Got Energy

In addition to her four books that *shout* energy and matter, Molly Bang's Caldecott Honor book, *When Sophie Gets Angry—Really, Really Angry*, offers readers a chance to see energy at work in a temper tantrum. Bang's vibrant reds and oranges communicate Sophie's anger when she doesn't want to share her stuffed gorilla. We can't help but notice her energy in the form of sound and motion as she runs screaming and kicking from the house. The cool colors seep into the illustrations as the tantrum subsides, and we can imagine the energy of her anger dissipating into the world. Bang's use of color is a familiar pattern for showing intensity. Heat maps, like the ones we see on weather or flu reports, show high intensity in bright reds, yellows, and oranges and low intensity in cooler colors.

the energy stored in the gasoline of our cars originated from the sun because oil (a fossil fuel) is actually liquefied ancient plants. Bang and Chisolm's books provide a foundation for understanding how the sun fuels everything, but in the following, we suggest how you might help your students trace energy back to the sun using any picture book.

Where did the energy come from? The answer is almost always the sun.

Find an illustration that shows something happening.	Follow the energy transfers from the sun.
A child is jumping rope.	Plants get their energy from the sun. Animals get their energy from eating plants. The child gets energy from eating plants and animals.
A bus is being driven	Plants that lived a long time ago were fueled by the sun. Those plants died and were compressed for millions of years, turning them into oil, coal, and natural gas (fossil fuels). The bus engine transfers the energy in the gas to the bus to make it go.
A tornado is forming.	The sun heats air that then rises. Warm air rises and cool air sinks causing unstable winds. The wind then spins at high speeds.
A child is flying a kite.	Flying a kite requires the wind to blow (same explanation as the tornado but on a smaller scale) and a child to hold the kite (follows the same path as jumping rope).
A power plant is producing hydroelectric power.	The sun evaporates water. The water falls as rain on a mountain top. The rain droplets flow into a river and eventually downstream through a turbine.

Books That Whisper Energy and Matter

Got Action?

Got action in the natural world? To explore the concept of energy in books that whisper, look for a book that presents a system in action; this is the energy out, and your clue for spotting it will always be the *-ing* form of verbs (running, jumping, eating, and so on), whether written in the text or pictured in the illustration. Ask your readers to describe what is happening in any illustration as an opportunity to discuss energy out. Red Riding Hood skipping down the forest path is using energy (kinetic) as motion to get to her grandmother's. The wolf, of course, is hiding and waiting to pounce (potential energy). Although not always shown, the energy in for any animal or person is always going to be their food, which as we know can be traced back to the sun. Hopefully the wolf is not using Little Red Riding Hood as his energy source.

In any book that involves Herculean feats (which often take the form of motion and sound), you can easily see energy transfer in the human realm. Look for books that celebrate the energy-driven accomplishments of athletes like runner Wilma Rudolph (*Wilma Unlimited: How Wilma Rudolph Became the World's Fastest Woman* [Krull]), baseball player Willie Mays (*Say Hey! A Song of Willie Mays* [Mandel]), or ballerina Anna Pavlova (*Swan: The Life and Dance of Anna Pavlova* [Snyder]). These individuals excelled at their sports because of their ability to transfer energy (energy out) to the track, ball, or dance floor. A book like *Fab Four Friends: The Boys Who Became the Beatles* (Reich) or *Woody Guthrie: Poet of the People* (Christensen) allows you to explore energy as singing (sound).

Two additional go-to topics for the natural world are weather and wind because they are present in many illustrations. A book like *Planting the Wild Garden* (Galbraith), or really any book that shows seed dispersal or leaves traveling on the wind, gives us the chance to talk about how energy is fueling this motion. On another page we see a rainstorm in the distance, which might provide an opportunity to discuss the energy in (sun) and energy out (falling rain, lightning, and thunder) of a storm system.

Got Plants?

With just a few exceptions, when you get down to it, organisms ultimately get their energy from the sun. The sun is the primary energy source for ecosystems and the process of photosynthesis is how the sun's energy enters these systems. We learn to appreciate the role of the sun and plants at an early age. You might ask your students, "How do plants get their energy?" to which they will almost certainly respond, "From the sun." Got plants? Any book that shows a plant growing and nods to the role of light offers an opportunity to discuss this topic because it shows energy in. During a read-aloud we shared an illustration of a plant in the sun and asked some third graders, "What would happen if we put this plant in the dark?" Zeke's response, "It won't have any energy, so it won't grow, and it will eventually die," shows that he knows sunlight is the fuel for plant growth.

We scanned our bookshelf for books that involved plants and picked out *In the Garden with Dr. Carver* (Grigsby). While flipping through this book, we noticed that we could ask "Got plants?" in several places. On one page we see Sally moving her floundering rosebush to a sunnier spot so it can grow (photosynthesize). This pattern of a healthy plant bathed in sunlight can be seen in the illustrations of countless picture books. On another page, the sun brightly lights a fence row framed by thriving pink flowers with a butterfly drinking nectar. An illustration like this whispers that energy is flowing through the system as it moves from sun to plant to butterfly.

Identify the system.	To reveal energy in, ask: "What is the fuel?"	To reveal energy out, ask: "What is the (system) doing?" Look for heat, sound, light, motion, electricity, or photosynthesis if the system is a plant.	To spot matter transformation, ask: "Is the (system) the same after the energy flowed through it?"
Organisms in action: A close look at one page in *Every Day Birds* (VanDerwater)			
A swooping owl	The fuel is the bird's food.	The owl is in flight (motion) and is a warm-blooded animal (heat). It may even hoot, in which case we are hearing energy out as sound.	The owl is not transformed by flying, keeping itself warm, or hooting.
Weather in action: A close look at one page in *I Know Here* (Croza)			
A forest of trees bent by the wind	The wind is providing the energy.	The trees are bending to the left as the wind blows across them.	The trees are not transformed by the wind.
Plants capturing energy: A close look at one page in *If You Love Honey* (Sullivan)			
A dandelion doing its work in the sun	The sun is the fuel.	The dandelion is photosynthesizing.	The plant is transformed through photosynthesis because it is growing.

Got Action in the Engineered World?

To consider energy in the engineered world, look for books about trains, planes, and automobiles (and bicycles or farm equipment), because they almost always feature energy transfer (lots of action) in the explanation of how they work. Because these are all systems that move and do things, they lend themselves to exploring kinetic energy. The fuel that powers these machines could easily lead to a discussion about potential energy. We chose *Big Tractor* (Clement) to illustrate how this might unfold in a discussion about any machine as shown below. (See Figure 7.4 for a beginning list of books that whisper energy and matter.)

TALK PROMPTS to help you spot the energy flow and matter transformation in a book about machinery			
Identify the system.	To reveal energy in, ask:"What is the fuel?"	To reveal energy out, ask: "What is the (system) doing?" Look for heat, sound, light, motion, or electricity.	To spot matter transformation, ask:"Is the (system) the same after the energy flowed through it?"
Big Tractor	The fuel is the diesel, which has potential energy until it combusts in the engine.	We can see that Big Tractor is mowing, cultivating, and preparing the soil: all forms of motion. Even though we can't hear the roar of the engine or feel its heat, we know energy is transferring out of this system in these forms as well.	Is the tractor the same? Yes, it is not transformed by using it. You might consider asking if the diesel was transformed. When Big Tractor burns the diesel, this fuel is transformed into exhaust (gases).

When Sophie Gets Angry—Really, Really Angry (Bang)

Home Run (Burleigh)

Big Tractor (Clement)

Speed (Clement)

Workshop (Clements)

Jack's Garden (Cole)

I Know Here (Croza)

The Popcorn Book (dePaola)

The Blue Whale (Desmond)

Planting the Wild Garden (Galbraith)

Something from Nothing (Gilman)

In the Garden with Dr. Carver (Grigsby)

My First Day (Jenkins and Page)

Henry Hikes to Fitchburg (Johnson)

The Prairie That Nature Built (Lorbiecki)

Seed Soil Sun: Earth's Recipe for Food (Peterson)

Blackout (Rocco)

The Streak (Rosenstock)

Swan: The Life and Dance of Anna Pavlova (Snyder)

Heat Wave (Spinelli)

If You Love Honey: Nature's Connections (Sullivan)

Joseph Had a Little Overcoat (Taback)

Every Day Birds (VanDerwater)

Figure 7.4

A beginning list of books that whisper energy and matter

Literary Fun with Energy and Matter

As Harry Potter fans, we enjoy the way that magic spells and potions can transform matter. Just as with cause and effect, it's fun to play outside the rules of physics and the natural world. Fantasy and folklore invite readers to think about how matter might transform. Shapeshifters, such as werewolves, selkies, and animagi, rely on mechanisms such as the phase of the moon or being in the water or on land as the signal to transform. Aladdin's lamp, magic wands or beans, and poison apples all can be grist for a lively discussion about energy transfer in an imaginary realm. In more realistic fiction, blizzards, hurricanes, and tornadoes—energy in motion—create scenarios and premises for conflict, hardship, and rebirth and recovery. Strong characters may also be a force. Would the Plaza Hotel be the same without Eloise's exuberant energy? She personifies energy transfer; the elevator stops at every floor because she pushes all the buttons. We know that energy in, energy out causes changes in systems. Even though it is not energy in a scientific sense, we often see characters transfer their emotional energy—perhaps fear, anger, or joy—to others, fueling the plot's twists and turns. In books like *Where the Wild Things Are* (Sendak), *Bridge to Terabithia* (Paterson), and *Each Kindness* (Woodson), we can see emotions as analogous to energy; they flow through the characters and affect their actions.

Listening for Literary Energy and Matter

Our daily language is infused with words and phrases that refer to energy, and you might want to keep a running list or anchor chart with your students as you discover them in daily conversation or reading. Some of our favorites include:

Let's get the ball rolling: Recognizing how energy appears in our daily discourse	
Word or phrase	Reference to energy
I'm trying to be efficient.	I'm trying to use less energy.
Stop wasting time.	Stop wasting energy.
Let's get the ball rolling. On your mark, get set, go.	Activate the potential energy.

Word or phrase	Reference to energy
Let's pick up the pace.	Let's put more energy into the system.
I need to lose weight.	I need to get rid of potential energy.
I'm spinning my wheels.	I'm wasting energy.
Wait for me.	Stop your kinetic energy.
I'm stuck. I'm waiting.	I have potential energy but I need activation energy.
May the force be with you.	May the energy transfer into you.
Go with the flow.	Don't fight the (kinetic) energy.
I'm procrastinating. I've got writer's block. I am trying to get over the hump.	I haven't found my activation energy.
Can we talk? I need to vent my anger.	I need to transfer my energy to your system.

8

STABILITY AND CHANGE

What's the New Normal?

Learning and Teaching the Science

What You Need to Know: *Systems Are Either Stable or Changing*

Dear Families,

A quick update on the repair of the broken water pipe at school. The pipe has been replaced and our custodial staff has been working with the State Water Supply Division to ensure that our school is following the protocol for safe water usage. Bottled water has been made available to students throughout the week and will continue through Friday when we anticipate normal water usage will resume.

Thank you for understanding,

Principal Teachout

Figure 8.1
In Olivia's drawing, the house is *stable*, but as the foot crushes it, the dollhouse will *change*.

This communiqué perfectly describes a system undergoing change heading back to equilibrium, and it's also the take-home message of this chapter: systems are in flux and at any moment are either stable or changing. For most systems, stability is the norm and we can see this in how a school operates daily. We expect everything to work, our schedules to be followed, and our students to be healthy, happy, and learning. Occasionally, during a snowstorm or flu outbreak (or when a pipe breaks), the system is temporarily *changing*, but it quickly returns to *stability* when the roads are plowed, the sick kids recover, or the pipe is fixed. (See Figure 8.1.)

Stability can take one of two forms: a system can either be in a state of *static equilibrium* or *dynamic equilibrium*. Take the pencil sharpener in your classroom as an example of a system. When it is not being used, it is a stable system that is in static equilibrium—nothing is happening in the system. When Anna sharpens her pencil, the system is in dynamic equilibrium because it's doing something. When she stops sharpening the pencil, the system returns to static equilibrium.

In contrast, your classroom is an example of a system in dynamic equilibrium. Something is happening all the time, but it is stable—there is no net change to the system—because the boundaries and interacting components that define the system do not change. The number of students in your class generally stays the same and you follow a routine. On Tuesday you have lunch at noon and on Thursdays literacy block begins at 9:30. This routine is predictable and is the pattern that defines your classroom system.

The key to spotting a system in dynamic equilibrium is remembering that something is happening but the system as a whole is not changing. To help your students understand static and dynamic equilibrium, ask them to compare a clock to a stapler. Both are stable systems but the clock is in dynamic equilibrium because the hands are always moving, but at the end of the day it is still the same clock. The stapler is also stable but it's in static equilibrium because it doesn't do anything until someone gives it a good whack. In our opening vignette, the school, usually in dynamic equilibrium, is undergoing change as a result of the burst pipe. When the pipe is repaired, the school will return to its cheerful dynamic equilibrium.

Whether static or dynamic, stable systems can change and changing systems can become stable. What causes this process? A change in the flow of matter and energy into a system. Pipes burst when they freeze. The amount of heat (energy) in the system has changed and water can no longer flow through them. When your students are experiencing a growth spurt, their bodies can be viewed as a changing system caused by the matter and energy flowing into them at every meal. A dormant volcano is a stable system but is undergoing change when erupting. To think like a scientist is to remember that a system is stable, changing, or both depending upon scale (see Figure 8.2). Changing systems typically move toward stability—their default state.

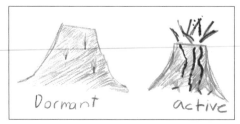

Figure 8.2

Wanda's drawing shows a volcano system in a dormant stable state and undergoing change when erupting.

Developing Your Lens: Scale Helps Us Spot When a System Is Stable or Changing

How can we tell when a system is stable or changing? It is all about scale and for most of your discussions, timescale will provide clues. Is a six-year-old child a stable or changing system? We all know that children are growing, but on a daily timescale, we expect our six-year-old to look and act in ways very similar to yesterday. The changes are imperceptible. When our six-year-old loses a tooth, however, we know the system is changing. In many cultures some form of tooth fairy comes at night to mark the occasion of a system undergoing change—a baby tooth is being replaced. Once the gaping hole is occupied by a healthy permanent tooth, the system has established a new normal but we know that this stability will be temporary because the child is still growing. For children, on the daily timescale, most days the system appears to be stable and in dynamic equilibrium, but when we zoom out to a year we can easily see that the system is changing. To think like a scientist is to recognize that many systems are both stable and changing depending on the scale you are using.

Timescale can also help you see your classroom as both a stable and changing system. During any given hour, there are the disruptions caused by an exuberant student, an intercom announcement, or a buzzing fly, which briefly change the system. Hearing, "One, two, three, eyes on me" hopefully brings the system to a stable state. On this hourly scale, the classroom system fluctuates from stability to change frequently. But if we zoom out to a weekly scale, we see these disruptions as part of a larger pattern that defines the dynamic equilibrium of this system. Just remember, scale will help you determine whether a system is currently stable or changing.

As pointed out above, natural systems like a growing child can be seen as both stable and undergoing change depending upon the timescale. Nonliving things in the natural world can also be seen as stable or changing. Most of the time volcanoes, mountains, and tectonic plates appear as stable to us and in static equilibrium; after all, significant eruptions, landslides, and earthquakes make international news because they are rare on the human timescale. On the geological timescale, these same events may define a changing system (Earth). When we observe storm clouds on the horizon, we know that today's weather will be changing very shortly, although this change is part of the dynamic equilibrium of our seasonal climate. The table below shows how a system may appear to be stable or undergoing change depending upon scale.

The same system can be in both dynamic equilibrium and undergoing change depending upon the scale		
What's the system and what are we observing or measuring?	Scale: What's the system doing at this scale?	Change the scale: Now what's the system doing?
Second grader and growth Scale: time	Day. We cannot see growth occur in this time frame; therefore the system is stable.	Decade. We can see the change in the system as ten years' worth of growth. In this time, the second grader has changed into a seventeen-year-old with a funky haircut.
Student attendance Scale: individual versus population	Individual. A student may be sick on Tuesday and have to miss school, which means the system (the absent student) is temporarily changing. When the student recovers, the system is returning to stability.	The school's student population. This system is stable even though on any given day a couple of students will be absent. Because the system as a whole is not changing, the system is stable. If a debilitating flu strikes the school causing mass absences, then the system would be temporarily undergoing change.
Weather pattern Scale: time	Seasonal. The weather pattern during the winter is predictably cooler than the summer. This is a stable pattern.	Century. Weather patterns are changing because of climate change.

In the engineered world, a changing system is undesirable, and the goal is to create stable systems that solve problems. We expect our bridges to stand, our buildings to bear the elements, and our vehicles to run smoothly. We know a poorly engineered system when we see one because it breaks, which is another way of saying the system is changing. This is why engineers use models and ask *what if* questions to test the limits of a system. Regular inspections of planes, bridges, elevators, and school buses ensure that these systems remain in a stable state—which is how we like them.

The Flow of Energy and Matter Affects Systems

Now that you recognize that systems often fluctuate between stability and change, the next step is to ask, "What's the mechanism for triggering change (or establishing stability)?" Consider the swings on your playground; when they are being used, energy is flowing through them. When the students return from recess, the swings return to their stable and static states because energy is no longer flowing through them. Furthermore, every system has a limit for the amount of energy and matter that can flow through it without causing the system to change. When three large teenagers return to their elementary school and try out the kiddie swings, the swings break because the system has surpassed its limits. Similarly, when the wind blows on a tree, the leaves rattle and the branches bend but the system tolerates the breeze. Make the breeze into a seventy-mile-per-hour gust and the system reaches its limit and will change as the boughs snap. Following, we offer examples of how the flow of energy and matter change a system.

The flow of energy and matter affects systems.

Stable system	Spot the flow of matter and energy into the system. Think cause.	How does the change in matter and energy affect the system? Think effect.
Energy and matter move systems of dynamic equilibrium into change.		
Classroom: Your classroom is undoubtedly lively but on a daily scale the boundaries and interacting components do not change, which means it is a stable system.	New matter and energy arrive in the form of a new student.	This new student joins the classroom, temporarily disrupting the stable system.
Classroom sink: Water flows in and out of the sink all day.	A paper towel (matter) gets stuck in the drain.	Until it's removed, the clog is disrupting the system by preventing the water from draining.
School bus: The bus arrives at 7:45 each morning.	The bus has run out of gas. It has no energy powering it.	The bus is running late.
Classroom heating and cooling system: The classroom stays at a constant temperature throughout the day.	A power outage prevents electricity from flowing through the system.	The HVAC system is no longer working.
Dormant volcano	Magma and hot gasses push to the surface.	The volcano is erupting. Air traffic is being halted.

Stable system	Spot the flow of matter and energy into the system. Think cause.	How does the change in matter and energy affect the system? Think effect.
Energy can move systems in static equilibrium into dynamic equilibrium or cause them to change.		
A book is resting on a table.	A student accidently rips a page out of the book.	The system is changing because the energy (the rip) has removed a page (matter) from the system.
Hula-Hoops during classes are at rest because they are not being used.	At recess students play with the hula hoops and transfer energy by swinging their hips.	The hula hoops are in dynamic equilibrium because they are moving.
The water fountain is still because it is not being used.	A student gets a drink by transferring energy to the handle.	The water fountain is in dynamic equilibrium because water is flowing through it.
A pebble is on the playground.	Energy is transferred to the pebble when the school's lawn mower whacks it with its blade, splitting it into tiny pieces.	The pebble is in change as it shatters into tiny pieces. Afterward, each piece will be a new and stable system.

We've all said, "I just want things to get back to normal," which is another way of saying, "I want this system to stabilize." You may be wondering how changing systems reach equilibrium. They do this when the energy and matter flowing into them stabilizes. All of the previous examples show stable systems changing or in dynamic equilibrium triggered by changes in energy and matter flowing into them. You can also read the table backward and see how removing energy or matter from a system creates a stable or static state. For example, start in the right column of the clogged drain and work backward to the left. The clogged drain will work again and become stable when the paper towel is removed, allowing water to flow in and out again. When the new student starts to make friends and learns the routines, we know that the classroom system has attained a new normal, or dynamic equilibrium.

Start by picking a system—all systems are either stable, changing, or both, depending upon scale.

Ask: "Is something happening in the system?"

If no, then the system is stable and in *static equilibrium.*

If yes, then ask: "Are the boundaries of the system or interacting components changing?" Remember to consider scale when answering this question.

No, the boundary and interacting components are not changing but something is happening in the system. This system is in *dynamic equilibrium.*

Yes, the boundaries and interacting components of the system are *changing.* Keep in mind that change is often short-lived and many systems soon return to *stability.* If not, we'd still be stuck in that traffic jam from thirty years ago.

Ask: "What is the energy or matter that caused the system to change?"

Exploring Stability and Change in Children's Literature

Books That Shout Stability and Change

It's easy to spot stability and change in nonfiction. Any life cycle book, like *Monarch and Milkweed* (Frost), *From Seed to Plant* (Gibbons), *An Island Grows* (Schaefer), or *Fire! The Renewal of a Forest* (Godkin), presents a system that cycles through stability and change. Biographies provide an opportunity to see how stability and change play out in a life. For example, *Just Behave, Pablo Picasso!* (Winter) highlights how Picasso's painting style brought change to what had been a period of stability in the art world. The narrative picture book about how the National Parks began, *The Camping Trip That Changed America* (Rosenstock), pivots around John Muir and Theodore Roosevelt's attempts to change the pattern of destroying wildlands. Basically, any book about natural systems will feature stability and change simply because all systems are either stable or changing.

Book Selection and Beginning Conversations

Because stability and change describe the state of a system, to explore this concept, pull out any book we suggested in Chapter 6 from the natural world that shouts systems and system models. Read the book to your students again. Because you have already identified the system's boundaries and interacting components, you can now guide your students to consider stability and change by noticing how energy and matter affect the system. Describe the dynamic equilibrium of the system, then help your students recognize change by identifying when or how the equilibrium is disrupted and what caused the disruption. Remember it will always be a change in the flow of matter and/or energy. Over time, this line of thinking will set readers up to notice change in any system.

To understand how a conversation like this might go, let's revisit the same books we explored in Chapter 6 that shout systems and system models, but this time we'll go a step further to consider whether the systems are stable or changing and identify the cause (flow of matter or energy).

TALK PROMPTS to explore whether systems are *stable* or *changing*

Book	Identify the system in the book.	Ask:"What's happening in this system?"	Ask:"Is it stable or changing?" If stable, ask: Is it in static or dynamic equilibrium?	If it is changing, ask:"What is the energy and/or matter that caused the system to change?"
When the Wolves Returned (Patent)	Yellowstone's ecosystem	Plants grow, herbivores eat the plants, and wolves eat the herbivores.	The system is changing because the introduction of the wolf alters the relationship between plants and herbivores, which in turn alters erosion.	The introduction of this carnivore alters how energy and matter flow through this ecosystem because the wolves eat the herbivores, which eat the plants, which then changes the course of the river.
The Honey Makers (Gibbons)	The beehive	Bees collect nectar, waggle, pollinate flowers, and make honey.	The system is stable and in dynamic equilibrium. A lot is happening in the hive, but the bees' activities follow a pattern.	This system is not changing in this book, but if a bear decided to help itself to the honey, the system would most definitely undergo change.

Disasters: Watch out for that iceberg!

Disaster is such a useful word because it describes unwanted changes to natural, engineered, or social systems. Natural disasters such as hurricanes, tornadoes, volcanoes, and earthquakes are appropriately called disasters because they can cause upheaval of historic proportion (scale!). Look for books about Pompeii, Hurricane Katrina, the tsunami of 2004, and even wars. We all know students who are fascinated with particular disasters; the sinking of the Titanic, the explosion of the Hindenburg, and the eruption of Mount St. Helens all come to mind. These events scream a huge and unexpected change in a system, which is one way to define disaster.

Topic Spotlight: Rivers

Rivers are a great topic for examining stability and change because these systems are typically stable and in dynamic equilibrium. As we all know, the water level rises and falls in a predictable manner that typically follows the seasons. Spring runoff and summer doldrums are a pattern. But a phrase like *one-hundred-year flood* instantly suggests that on the scale of a human lifetime, the system is changing at a historic proportion. After a flood, a river will return to its bed or a newly created one, settling into dynamic equilibrium. Share a book like *Nora's Ark* (Kinsey-Warnock) to explore stability and change with your class. A book like this explains what happens to a river after nine inches of rain. Illustrations show farm animals being brought into living rooms, a cow precariously wedged in a tree, and a barn and other flotsam floating downstream. After three days, the river forms a stable albeit new dynamic equilibrium. Stories like these are a powerful way to explore change and stability because they show how a disruption to the stability of a natural system can change lives, society, engineered structures, the landscape, and even your favorite swimming hole. (See Figure 8.3 for a list of books about rivers.)

A River Ran Wild (Cherry)

Abe Lincoln Crosses a Creek (Hopkinson)

Nora's Ark (Kinsey-Warnock)

River Friendly, River Wild (Kurtz)

The Raft (LaMarche)

Where the River Begins (Locker)

Canoe Days (Paulsen)

Three Days on a River in a Red Canoe (Williams)

Letting Swift River Go (Yolen)

Figure 8.3

Some river titles to get you afloat

Books That Whisper Stability and Change

Stability and change is another crosscutting concept that doubles as a literary device. In fiction, plotlines cycle through periods of stability and change with every twist and turn of the plot. When authors present their story "system," they may start with a stable setting and characters in equilibrium (it's a typical day) followed by an outside influence that disrupts the system. E. B. White sets this up perfectly in the opening of *Charlotte's Web*. "'Where's Papa going with that ax?' said Fern to her mother as they were setting the table for breakfast." Astute readers suspect that the ax is about to disrupt the breakfast routine in some way. Stability is reestablished when Wilbur is safely settled in the barnyard, but when the goose reveals that pigs become bacon, the system is changing yet again.

As readers, we notice how story systems made up of characters and settings fluctuate between stability and change in books. In literary terms, we might call this fluctuation rising and falling action. In short picture books, there may be one noticeable change with a return to stability, but the numerous chapters of a novel such as *Charlotte's Web* allow room for plot twists that provide the reader with a wild ride through many fluctuations of stability and change.

Humans are social creatures, and we thrive in social systems like families, schools, clubs, and teams, and it is easy to spot stability and change in the many books about these systems found in children's literature. Next, we show how we identified the social system with a few books we pulled off our shelf. Try asking these questions with any book that has a social system as a driving force in the plot.

TALK PROMPTS to help you spot stability and change in any book about a social system			
Book and System	Ask: "What is normal like in this system?" This will help your students see the pattern that defines the system when it's stable.	Ask: "What causes it to change?" For systems in the science realm, keep an eye out for energy and matter.	Ask: "What's the new norm?" This will help your students see that the system has regained stability but with a new dynamic.
Miss Nelson Is Missing! (Allard) System: the classroom	The class is unruly and disrespectful.	Miss Nelson disappears and the substitute (Miss Viola Swamp, who is Miss Nelson in disguise) throws the system into disarray.	The students appreciate Miss Nelson after a day with Miss Viola Swamp and change their classroom behavior.
The Lady in the Box (McGovern) System: the woman's homelessness	The woman is homeless, cold, and hungry. At the moment, her tragic situation is unfortunately stable and not yet changing.	The children bring the woman food and clothes.	The children's mother helps get the woman to a shelter to begin a new life. Her system is changing and will soon become a new and stable norm.

continues

Book and System	Ask: "What is normal like in this system?" This will help your students see the pattern that defines the system when it's stable.	Ask: "What causes it to change?" For systems in the science realm, keep an eye out for energy and matter.	Ask: "What's the new norm?" This will help your students see that the system has regained stability but with a new dynamic.
Owen and Mzee: The True Story of a Remarkable Friendship (Hatkoff, Hatkoff, and Kahumbu) System: Family	Owen is a young hippo that is living happily with his mother in Kenya.	A flood and the tsunami of 2004 separate Owen from his mother when he is washed out to sea and then washes ashore elsewhere.	Owen adopts Mzee, a 130-year-old tortoise, as his parent, establishing a new family system for himself.
This Is Not My Hat (Klassen) System: Hat ownership	The big fish has a hat and the little fish does not.	The little fish stole a hat from the big sleeping fish and is hurriedly swimming for safety in the weeds. Everybody is agitated.	The final illustrations show the big fish swimming into the weeds and then leaving with the hat. What happens in between is left to our imagination. Once the big fish gets the hat back, the system forms a new stability. We do not know what happens to the little fish. Perhaps it was eaten or maybe had agreeably returned the hat to the larger fish. Endings that do not explicitly reveal how the system returns to stability are often intriguing because we are left with unanswered questions. Now we are agitated.

We all know that some changes are more significant than others—it's a matter of scale. Here in Vermont, we swap out our regular tires and snow tires twice a year. It's a small change to our cars (the system) that makes our daily driving a little different. When we get married, that is a bigger change and we might even call it a personal milestone. Our lives are forever changed as a result. Historical moments change the much larger system of society. As we illustrate in the following, the common theme to each of these is a stable system that is thrown into change and then the system reestablishes stability.

Today Was a Little Different . . .

Our daily lives are filled with brief moments of change. A student may stay home one day with a cold, and on another day, be greeted at the classroom door by a substitute teacher. Once a year, we have a birthday that briefly changes our routine. Holidays come and go and occasionally we have a snow day. On the daily timescale, these are small changes to the stability of our system and we quickly return to our norm. Your classroom library is filled with books that present these small changes. Look for books on birthdays, winning the game, getting lost, field trips, or substitute teachers—anything that signals a change in a daily routine will work. A book like *Alexander and the Terrible, Horrible, No Good, Very Bad Day* (Viorst) chronicles what happens when Alexander loses his temper, which changes the dynamic equilibrium of this family system.

Personal Milestones

Personal milestones have a big impact on an individual even if they don't affect society. What keeps a classic like *Julius, the Baby of the World* (Henkes) in print is that a new sibling is a universal change to a family system that many of your students have experienced. Life-changing events, both good and bad, are often the focus of children's books, particularly in middle and upper elementary grades. Numerous picture books convey the emotional power of divorce, blending families, moving to a new home or school, or the loss of a pet.

Historical Moments

We can think of historical moments as society's milestones. These events throw the current system into change. Our generation may remember where we were on 9/11, and past generations recall when they learned President John F. Kennedy had been shot. Many books describe a pivotal moment in history. Readers will recognize two common trajectories in these. Authors either start with the stable state (it is a normal day) and then explain the cause of the change (an earthquake strikes), or they begin with the changing system (Civil War) and explain how stability is reestablished with a new norm (Civil Rights). This, of course, is why we call them historical moments, because our culture and society are permanently transformed into a new form of stability as a result of the system changing. In regaining stability, cities may be rebuilt after fires and natural disasters, borders may be redrawn after wars, and new constituencies may be given the right to vote.

Many historical narratives offer readers the chance to see a system moving between stability and change. *Fireboat* (Kalman) begins in the 1930s with the story of a New York City boat doings its job on a bustling Hudson River. This fireboat plays a small yet crucial role in the city's dynamic equilibrium. By the 1990s the aging fireboat has been relegated to hobby status

TODAY WAS A LITTLE DIFFERENT	HISTORICAL MOMENTS
When Sophie Gets Angry—Really, Really Angry (Bang)	*Papa's Mechanical Fish* (Fleming)
The Tub People (Conrad)	*Drylongso* (Hamilton)
Strega Nona (DePaola)	*How the Meteorite Got to the Museum* (Hartland)
Too Many Toys (Shannon)	*Rachel Carson and Her Book That Changed the World* (Lawlor)
Madlenka (Sís)	*The Camping Trip That Changed America* (Rosenstock)
Alexander and the Terrible, Horrible, No Good, Very Bad Day (Viorst)	*An Island Grows* (Schaefer)
PERSONAL MILESTONES	*The Day Gogo Went to Vote* (Sisulu)
Fred Stays with Me! (Coffelt)	*Elizabeth Leads the Way: Elizabeth Cady Stanton and the Right to Vote* (Stone)
I Know Here (Croza)	*Just Behave, Pablo Picasso!* (Winter)
Emily's Blue Period (Daly)	
Julius, the Baby of the World (Henkes)	
A Storm Called Katrina (Uhlberg)	
A Place Where Hurricanes Happen (Watson)	
Klara's New World (Winter)	

Figure 8.4

A beginning list of books that whisper stability and change

for dilettantes. When the twin towers are struck by airplanes and the water pipes are broken, the system is thrown into change. The story concludes with the role this boat played in helping to extinguish the flames on that historic day. Books like this provide you and your students an opportunity to see how change in systems influences their lives, society, and history. (See Figure 8.4 for a beginning list of books that whisper stability and change.)

Listening for Literary Stability and Change

Words that describe patterns scream stability, and expressions that refer to the breaking of a pattern, such as, "We're in crisis mode," often indicate change. Here are some of the ones we have noticed in our daily discussions, and we are sure that you and your students will have fun adding to this list.

What's the new normal?

Recognizing how the fluctuations of stability and change appear in our daily discourse

Language	Reference to stability or change
Emergency! Emptying Flood of ideas I just want things to return to normal Once in a lifetime Overflowing Upheaval We're in crisis mode Your cup runneth over You're in trouble Historical moment The flag is at half-mast We're renovating the school	The system is changing.
Her heart rate has returned to normal It's the new normal Regular Routine Schedule Status quo Today we will follow a normal Friday Typical day Version 2.0 Well-child checkup	The system has returned to stability or created a new stability.
Calm down Focus Take a deep breath Take a break	We need to stabilize the system.
Adding fuel to the fire Disrupt Fanning the flames Hit the reboot button I'm reaching the boiling point I've reached my limit Jam packed Leveling up Standing room only	The system is about to change.
Don't burst my bubble Don't mess with me I like it the way it is	Don't change my system.

Metaphors help us see stability and change in language, and they can also help us find titles of books about change. Although rare, we found several titles that actually have the word *change* in them, like *Rachel Carson and Her Book That Changed the World* (Lawlor) or *The Camping Trip That Changed America* (Rosenstock). Other titles suggest change through rare or singular events like *Baseball <u>Saved</u> Us* (Mochizuki), *That <u>Bothered</u> Kate* (Noll), *<u>Attack</u> on Pearl Harbor* (Tanaka), and *The Wednesday <u>Surprise</u>* (Bunting). Look for words that hint at change such as *surprise, good-bye, learn, returned, gone, leave,* or *new.* Titles that nod at energy or matter flow are also good bets such as *Crashed, Smashed, and Mashed: A Trip to Junkyard Heaven* (Mitchell). We can see how the expressions *jam-packed* or *I've reached my limit* could translate into a book title like *<u>Too Many</u> Toys* (Shannon). All of these titles clearly set up the reader to expect a story about a system in change.

You've now read this book and shared many others with your class to make the crosscutting concepts part of your lens. We're sure that you're ready for recess (we are). Fortunately for your students, the playground is an ideal system for seeing how these seven concepts are everywhere. Ready? Turn the page.

AFTERWORD

Are You Ready for the Championship of Crosscutting Concepts? It Takes Place at Recess!

After reading and discussing the crosscutting concepts, your students are no doubt developing their scientific lenses and observing that the crosscutting concepts are intertwined. In your read-alouds and discussions, you've probably noticed that some books lend themselves equally well to discussions of multiple concepts. In writing this book, some of our favorite aha moments occurred as we wrote subsequent chapters and discovered how cumulative and interwoven the concepts truly are. For example, as we were writing the chapter on stability and change, we realized that the book *Blackout* (Rocco) that we used to highlight cause and effect would also be a perfect place to discuss systems—both the social system of the family and the electrical grid as an engineered system. Many of Steve Jenkins' books invite discussion about both structure and function and cause and effect. This, of course, is why these concepts are called *crosscutting*. Once you have the mindset of thinking like a scientist, you see them everywhere.

Beyond your classroom or school library, you have a perfect system for exploring the crosscutting concepts on your school grounds: your playground! Take a couple of minutes at recess to pull your students aside and have them describe the playground before anyone is on it. It is a stable system at rest (static equilibrium), and when the students rush onto the swings, slides, and monkey bars, the system will be in dynamic equilibrium as the energy and matter of the students flow through the playground causing things to happen. Lila will swing, Reuben will climb, and Ava will slide, while some first graders head over to the sandbox to build a model amusement park for ants. How do you know a slide or swing when you see one? Because each of these systems is defined by a pattern. The chains and seats that make up the swings are the structures that allow the function of swinging. Kindergartner Cole is swinging high for him, but he's so low relative to a fourth grader that it causes her to ask him if he needs a push. What she's really asking is, "Would you like for me to transfer some energy to you?"

This is what it means to think like a scientist—to actively see the crosscutting concepts as we make sense of our physical world. Playgrounds are a rich topic for exploration because there are many entry points for identifying the crosscutting concepts. We use the slide, as shown below, but the monkey bars or climbing ropes will get you there, too.

- Pattern: How do you know a slide when you see one? The ladder, smooth shiny surface, and railing are recognizable repeats that shout slide.

- Cause and effect: The students are sliding because they climbed up to the top of the structure. The mechanism is gravity.

- Structure and function: The shape and physical properties of the slide and Ava's clothing allow her to rocket down this structure.

- Scale: The slide is tall for the first graders but not for the fourth graders.

- System and system models: The slide is a system because it has interacting components and a boundary.

- Energy and matter: The arrival of energetic students to the playground causes things to happen. Legs climb and arms pull students up the ladder. The slide is now a system in dynamic equilibrium.

- Stability and change: When the students return to their classrooms, the slide returns to static equilibrium. When the PTA replaces the slide next year, it will change and then be the new normal.

CHILDREN'S LITERATURE CITED

Aardema, Verna. 1975. *Why Mosquitoes Buzz in People's Ears: A West African Tale*. Illustrated by Leo Dillon and Diane Dillon. New York: Dial Press.

Allard, Harry. 1977. *Miss Nelson Is Missing!* Illustrations by James Marshall. Boston: Houghton Mifflin.

Arnold, Caroline. 2003. *Birds: Nature's Magnificent Flying Machines*. Illustrated by Patricia Wynne. Watertown, MA: Charlesbridge.

Aston, Dianna Hutts. 2007. *A Seed Is Sleepy*. Illustrated by Sylvia Long. San Francisco: Chronicle Books.

Balliett, Blue. 2008. *The Calder Game*. Illustrated by Brett Helquist. New York: Scholastic.

Bang, Molly. 1994. *One Fall Day*. New York: Greenwillow Books.

———. 1998. *When Sophie Gets Angry—Really, Really, Angry*. New York: Blue Sky Press.

———. 2004. *My Light*. New York: Blue Sky Press.

Bang, Molly, and Penny Chisholm. 2009. *Living Sunlight: How Plants Bring the Earth to Life*. Illustrated by Molly Bang. New York: Blue Sky Press.

———. 2012. *Ocean Sunlight: How Tiny Plants Feed the Seas*. Illustrated by Molly Bang. New York: Blue Sky Press.

———. 2014. *Buried Sunlight: How Fossil Fuels Have Changed the Earth*. Illustrated by Molly Bang. New York: Blue Sky Press.

Banks, Kate. 2006. *Max's Words*. Illustrated by Boris Kulikov. New York: Farrar, Straus, and Giroux.

Banyai, Istvan. 1995. *Zoom*. New York: Viking.

Barnett, Mac. 2014. *Sam and Dave Dig a Hole*. Illustrated by Jon Klassen. London: Walker Books.

Baylor, Byrd. 1974. *Everybody Needs a Rock*. Illustrated by Peter Parnall. New York: C. Scribner's Sons.

Bean, Jonathan. 2013. *Building Our House*. New York: Farrar, Straus, and Giroux.

Bernard, Robin. 2001. *A Tree for All Seasons*. Washington, DC: National Geographic Society.

Bluemle, Elizabeth. 2014. *Tap Tap Boom Boom*. Illustrated by G. Brian Karas. Cambridge, MA: Candlewick Press.

Brenner, Barbara. 2004. *One Small Place in a Tree*. Illustrated by Tom Leonard. New York: HarperCollins.

Brett, Jan. 1989. *The Mitten: A Ukrainian Folktale*. New York: Putnam.

Brisson, Pat. 1994. *Wanda's Roses*. Illustrated by Maryann Cocca-Leffler. Honesdale, PA: Caroline House, Boyds Mills Press.

———. 2014. *Before We Eat: From Farm to Table*. Illustrated by Mary Azarian. Thomaston, ME: Tilbury House.

Browne, Anthony. 2001. *My Dad*. New York: Farrar, Straus, and Giroux.

Bryant, Jennifer. 2014. *The Right Word: Roget and His Thesaurus*. Illustrated by Melissa Sweet. Grand Rapids, MI: Eerdsmans Books for Young Readers.

Bunting, Eve. 1989. *The Wednesday Surprise*. Illustrated by Donald Carrick. New York: Clarion Books.

———. 1991. *Fly Away Home*. Illustrated by Ronald Himler. New York: Clarion Books.

———. 2006a. *One Green Apple*. Illustrated by Ted Lewin. New York: Clarion Books.

———. 2006b. *Pop's Bridge*. Illustrated by C. F. Payne. Orlando: Harcourt.

Burleigh, Robert. 1998. *Home Run: The Story of Babe Ruth*. Illustrated by Mike Wimmer. San Diego: Silver Whistle.

Burton, Virginia Lee. 1942. *The Little House*. Boston: Houghton Mifflin.

Carle, Eric. 1986. *Papa, Please Get the Moon for Me*. New York: Simon & Schuster.

———. 1987a. *The Tiny Seed*. Natick, MA: Picture Book Studio.

——— 1987b. *The Very Hungry Caterpillar*. New York: Philomel Books.

Chaucer, Geoffrey, and Nevill Coghill. 2003. *The Canterbury Tales*. London: Penguin Books.

Cherry, Lynne. 1992. *A River Ran Wild: An Environmental History*. San Diego: Harcourt Brace Jovanovich.

Christelow, Eileen. 1993. *The Five-Dog Night*. New York: Clarion Books.

Christensen, Bonnie. 2001. *Woody Guthrie: Poet of the People*. New York: Knopf.

Clement, Nathan. 2013. *Speed*. Honesdale, PA: Boyds Mills Press.

———. 2015. *Big Tractor*. Honesdale, PA: Boyds Mills Press.

Clements, Andrew. 1998. *Workshop*. Illustrated by David Wisniewski. New York: Clarion Books.

Coffelt, Nancy. 2007. *Fred Stays with Me!* Illustrated by Tricia Tusa. New York: Little, Brown.

Cole, Henry. 1995. *Jack's Garden*. New York: Greenwillow Books.

Collard, Sneed B. 2008. *Teeth*. Illustrated by Phyllis V. Saroff. Watertown, MA: Charlesbridge.

Collins, Suzanne. 2010. *The Hunger Games*. London: Scholastic.

Conrad, Pam. 1989. *The Tub People*. Illustrated by Richard Egielski. New York: Harper & Row.

Cooney, Barbara. 1982. *Miss Rumphius*. New York: Viking.

Crichton, Michael. 2012. *Jurassic Park*. New York: Ballantine Books.

Cronin, Doreen. 2003. *Diary of a Worm*. Illustrated by Harry Bliss. New York: Joanna Cotler Books.

Croza, Laurel. 2013. *I Know Here*. Illustrated by Matt James. Toronto: Groundwood Books/ House of Anansi Press.

Dahl, Roald. 1961. *James and the Giant Peach*. Illustrated by Nancy Ekholm Burkert. New York: A. A. Knopf.

Daly, Cathleen. 2014. *Emily's Blue Period*. Illustrated by Lisa Brown. New York: Roaring Brook Press.

Davies, Nicola. 2012. *Outside Your Window: A First Book of Nature*. Illustrated by Mark Hearld. Somerville, MA: Candlewick Press.

———. 2014. *Tiny Creatures: The World of Microbes*. Illustrated by Emily Sutton. Somerville, MA: Candlewick Press.

Davis, Kathryn. 2014. *Mr. Ferris and His Wheel*. Illustrated by Gilbert Ford. Boston: HMH Books for Young Readers.

Daywalt, Drew. 2013. *The Day the Crayons Quit*. Illustrated by Oliver Jeffers. New York: Philomel.

DePaola, Tomie. 1975. *Strega Nona: An Old Tale*. Englewood Cliffs, NJ: Prentice-Hall.

———. 1978. *The Popcorn Book*. New York: Holiday House.

Desmond, Jenni. 2015. *The Blue Whale*. Brooklyn, NY: Enchanted Lion Books.

DiTerlizzi, Andrea. 2014. *Some Bugs*. San Diego: Beach Lane Books.

Doherty, Craig A., and Katherine M. Doherty. 1995. *The Golden Gate Bridge*. Woodbridge, CT: Blackbirch Press.

Drummond, Allan. 2011. *Energy Island: How One Community Harnessed the Wind and Changed Their World*. New York: Farrar, Straus, and Giroux.

———. 2016. *Green City: How One Community Survived a Tornado and Rebuilt for a Sustainable Future*. St. Louis: Turtleback Books.

Fanelli, Sara. 1995. *My Map Book*. New York: HarperCollins.

Finger, Brad. 2015. *13 Bridges Children Should Know*. New York: Prestel.

Fleischman, Paul. 2013. *The Matchbox Diary*. Illustrated by Bagram Ibatoulline. Cambridge, MA: Candlewick.

Fleming, Candace. 2013. *Papa's Mechanical Fish*. Illustrated by Boris Kulikov. New York: Margaret Ferguson Books.

Fleming, Denise. 1991. *In the Tall, Tall Grass*. New York: Henry Holt.

———. 1993. *In the Small, Small Pond*. New York: Henry Holt.

Fogliano, Julie. 2012. *And Then It's Spring*. Illustrated by Erin E. Stead. New York: Roaring Brook Press.

Fowler, Susi Gregg. 1994. *I'll See You When the Moon Is Full*. Illustrated by Jim Fowler. New York: Greenwillow Books.

Franco, Betsy. 2008. *Bees, Snails, & Peacock Tails: Patterns & Shapes—Naturally*. Illustrated by Steve Jenkins. New York: Margaret K. McElderry Books.

Frost, Helen. 2008. *Monarch and Milkweed*. Illustrated by Leonid Gore. New York: Atheneum Books for Young Readers.

Galbraith, Kathryn Osebold. 2011. *Planting the Wild Garden*. Illustrated by Wendy Anderson Halperin. Atlanta: Peachtree Publishers.

George, Jean Craighead. 2008. *The Wolves Are Back*. Illustrated by Wendell Minor. New York: Dutton Children's Books.

Gerber, Carole. 2013. *Seeds, Bees, Butterflies, and More! Poems for Two Voices*. Illustrated by Eugene Yelchin. New York: Henry Holt.

Gerstein, Mordicai. 1998. *The Wild Boy*. New York: Farrar, Straus, and Giroux.

———. 2003. *The Man Who Walked Between the Towers*. Brookfield, CT: Roaring Brook Press.

Gibbons, Gail. 1987. *Zoo*. New York: T. Y. Crowell.

———. 1989. *Monarch Butterfly*. New York: Holiday House.

———. 1991. *From Seed to Plant*. New York: Holiday House.

———. 1993. *Weather Forecasting*. New York: Macmillan.

———. 1994. *Emergency!* New York: Holiday House.

———. 1995a. *Planet Earth/Inside Out*. New York: Morrow Junior Books.

———. 1995b. *The Reasons for Seasons*. New York: Holiday House.

———. 1997. *The Honey Makers*. New York: Morrow Junior Books.

———. 2002. *Tell Me, Tree: All About Trees for Kids*. Boston: Little, Brown.

———. 2009a. *Hurricanes!* New York: Holiday House.

———. 2009b. *Tornadoes!* New York: Holiday House.

———. 2012. *How a House Is Built*. New York: Holiday House.

———. 2015. *It's Raining!* New York: Holiday House.

Gilman, Phoebe. 1992. *Something from Nothing*. New York: Scholastic.

Godkin, Celia. 2006. *Fire! The Renewal of a Forest*. Markham, ON: Fitzhenry & Whiteside.

Goldstone, Bruce. 2012. *Awesome Autumn*. New York: Henry Holt.

Goodman, Emily. 2009. *Plant Secrets*. Illustrated by Phyllis Limbacher Tildes. Watertown, MA: Charlesbridge.

Gray, Rita. 2015. *Flowers Are Calling*. Illustrated by Kenard Pak. Boston: HMH Books for Young Readers.

Grigsby, Susan. 2013. *In the Garden with Dr. Carver*. Illustrated by Nicole Tadgell. New York: Albert Whitman & Co.

Halfmann, Janet. 2012. *Eggs 1, 2, 3: Who Will the Babies Be?* Illustrated by Betsy Thompson. Maplewood, NJ: Blue Apple Books.

Hamilton, Virginia. 1992. *Drylongso*. Illustrated by Jerry Pinkney. San Diego: Harcourt Brace
    Jovanovich.

Hartland, Jessie. 2013. *How the Meteorite Got to the Museum*. Maplewood, NJ: Blue
    Apple Books.

Hatkoff, Isabella, Craig Hatkoff, and Paula Kahumbu. 2006. *Owen & Mzee: The True Story
    of a Remarkable Friendship*. Photographs by Peter Greste. New York: Scholastic.

Henderson, Kathy. 2004. *And the Good Brown Earth*. Cambridge, MA: Candlewick Press.

Henkes, Kevin. 1990. *Julius, the Baby of the World*. New York: Greenwillow Books.

———. 1991. *Chrysanthemum*. New York: Greenwillow Books.

———. 2015. *Waiting*. New York: Greenwillow Books.

Hopkins, Joseph H. 2013. *The Tree Lady*. Illustrated by Jill McElmurry. New York: Beach
    Lane Books.

Hopkinson, Deborah. 2008. *Abe Lincoln Crosses a Creek: A Tall, Thin Tale (introducing
    His Forgotten Frontier Friend)*. Illustrated by John Hendrix. New York: Schwartz &
    Wade Books.

Hosford, Kate. 2012. *Infinity and Me*. Illustrated by Gabi Swiatkowska. Minneapolis:
    Carolrhoda Books.

Hubbell, Patricia. 2008. *Airplanes: Soaring! Diving! Turning!* New York: Marshall Cavendish.

———. 2009. *Boats: Speeding! Sailing! Cruising!* New York: Marshall Cavendish.

Hurley, Michael. 2012. *The World's Most Amazing Bridges*. Chicago: Raintree.

Hutchins, Pat. 1986. *The Doorbell Rang*. New York: Greenwillow Books.

James, Robert. 2012. *How the Elephant Got Its Trunk*. Illustrated by Garyfallia Leftheri. New
    York: Crabtree Publishing.

James, Simon. 1991. *My Friend Whale*. New York: Bantam Books.

Jenkins, Steve. 1995. *Biggest, Strongest, Fastest*. New York: Ticknor & Fields Books for Young
    Readers.

———. 1998. *Hottest, Coldest, Highest, Deepest*. Boston: Houghton Mifflin.

———. 2004. *Actual Size*. Boston: Houghton Mifflin.

———. 2005. *Prehistoric Actual Size*. Boston: Houghton Mifflin.

———. 2007. *Living Color*. Boston: Houghton Mifflin.

———. 2010. *Bones: Skeletons and How They Work*. New York: Scholastic Reference.

———. 2011. *Just a Second: A Different Way to Look at Time*. Boston: Houghton Mifflin Books
    for Children.

Jenkins, Steve, and Robin Page. 2001. *Animals in Flight*. Boston: Houghton Mifflin.

———. 2003. *What Do You Do with a Tail Like This?* Boston: Houghton Mifflin.

———. 2006. *Move!* Boston: Houghton Mifflin.

———. 2008a. *How Many Ways Can You Catch a Fly?* Boston: Houghton Mifflin.

———. 2008b. *Sisters and Brothers: Sibling Relationships in the Animal World.* Boston: Houghton Mifflin.

———. 2011. *Time to Eat.* Boston: Houghton Mifflin Books for Children.

———. 2013. *My First Day.* Boston: Houghton Mifflin Books for Children.

———. 2014. *Creature Features: 25 Animals Explain Why They Look the Way They Do.* Boston: HMH Books for Young Readers.

Johmann, Carol A., and Elizabeth J. Rieth. 1999. *Bridges! Amazing Structures to Design, Build, and Test.* Illustrated by Michael P. Kline. Charlotte, VT: Williamson.

Johnson, Angela. 2007. *Wind Flyers.* Illustrated by Loren Long. New York: Simon & Schuster Books for Young Readers.

Johnson, D. B. 2000. *Henry Hikes to Fitchburg.* Boston: Houghton Mifflin.

Johnson, Rebecca L. 2015. *When Lunch Fights Back: Wickedly Clever Animal Defenses.* Minneapolis: Millbrook Press.

Johnston, Tony. 1994. *Amber on the Mountain.* Illustrated by Robert Duncan. New York: Dial Books for Young Readers.

Judge, Lita. 2010. *Born to Be Giants: How Baby Dinosaurs Grew to Rule the World.* New York: Flash Point.

Juster, Norton. 2005. *The Hello, Goodbye Window.* Illustrated by Christopher Raschka. New York: Michael Di Capua Books/Hyperion Books for Children.

Kalman, Maira. 2002. *Fireboat: The Heroic Adventures of the John J. Harvey.* New York: G. P. Putnam's Sons.

Kamkwamba, William, and Bryan Mealer. 2012. *The Boy Who Harnessed the Wind.* Illustrated by Elizabeth Zunon. New York: Dial Press.

Kinsey-Warnock, Natalie. 2005. *Nora's Ark.* Illustrated by Emily Arnold McCully. New York: HarperCollins.

Kipling, Rudyard. 2004. *A Collection of Rudyard Kipling's Just So Stories.* Cambridge, MA: Candlewick Press.

Klassen, Jon. 2012. *This Is Not My Hat.* Somerville, MA: Candlewick Press.

Kleven, Elisa. 2007. *The Puddle Pail.* Berkeley, CA: Tricycle Press.

Klise, Kate. 1998. *Regarding the Fountain: A Tale, in Letters, of Liars and Leaks.* Illustrated by M. Sarah Klise. New York: Avon Books.

———. 2001. *Trial by Journal.* New York: HarperCollins.

Krull, Kathleen. 1996. *Wilma Unlimited: How Wilma Rudolph Became the World's Fastest Woman.* Illustrated by David Diaz. San Diego: Harcourt Brace.

Kurtz, Jane. 2000. *River Friendly, River Wild*. Illustrated by Neil Brennan. New York: Simon & Schuster Books for Young Readers.

LaMarche, Jim. 2000. *The Raft*. New York: HarperCollins.

Landau, Elaine. 2011. *Oil Spill! Disaster in the Gulf of Mexico*. Minneapolis: Millbrook Press.

Lawlor, Laurie. 2012. *Rachel Carson and Her Book That Changed the World*. Illustrated by Laura Beingessner. New York: Holiday House.

Leedy, Loreen. 2010. *The Shocking Truth About Energy*. New York: Holiday House.

Lerner, Carol. 2002. *Butterflies in the Garden*. New York: HarperCollins.

Levenson, George. 1999. *Pumpkin Circle: The Story of a Garden*. Illustrated by Shmuel Thaler. Berkeley, CA: Tricycle Press.

Levine, Ellen. 2007. *Henry's Freedom Box*. Illustrated by Kadir Nelson. New York: Scholastic.

Lionni, Leo. 1960. *Inch by Inch*. New York: I. Obolensky.

Locker, Thomas. 1984. *Where the River Begins*. New York: Dial Books.

———. 1997. *Water Dance*. San Diego: Harcourt Brace & Company.

Lorbiecki, Marybeth. 2014. *The Prairie That Nature Built*. Illustrated by Cathy Morrison. Nevada City, CA: Dawn Publications.

Lowry, Lois. 1989. *Number the Stars*. Boston: Houghton Mifflin.

Lynch, Wayne. 2003. *Whose Teeth Are These?* Milwaukee: Gareth Stevens Publishing.

Lyon, George Ella. 2011. *All the Water in the World*. Illustrated by Katherine Tillotson. New York: Atheneum Books for Young Readers.

Macaulay, David. 1973. *Cathedral: The Story of Its Construction*. Boston: Houghton Mifflin.

———. 1977. *Castle*. Boston: Houghton Mifflin.

———. 1988. *The Way Things Work*. Boston: Houghton Mifflin.

———. 2003. *Mosque*. Boston: Houghton Mifflin.

Macken, JoAnn Early. 2008. *Flip, Float, Fly: Seeds on the Move*. Illustrated by Pamela Paparone. New York: Holiday House.

———. 2009. *Building a Bridge*. Mankato, MN: Capstone Press.

Mandel, Peter. 2000. *Say Hey! A Song of Willie Mays*. Illustrated by Don Tate. New York: Jump at the Sun/Hyperion Books for Children.

Mann, Elizabeth. 1996. *The Brooklyn Bridge: A Wonders of the World Book*. Illustrated by Alan Witschonke. New York: Mikaya Press.

Markle, Sandra. 2013. *What If You Had Animal Teeth!?* Illustrated by Howard McWilliam. New York: Scholastic.

Martin, Bill Jr. 1992. *Brown Bear, Brown Bear, What Do You See?* Illustrated by Eric Carle. New York: Henry Holt.

McGovern, Ann. 1997. *The Lady in the Box*. Illustrated by Marnie Backer. New York: Turtle Books.

McLerran, Alice. 1991. *Roxaboxen*. Illustrated by Barbara Cooney. New York: Lothrop, Lee & Shepard.

McNulty, Faith. 1986. *The Lady and the Spider*. Illustrated by Bob Marstall. New York: Harper & Row.

Menzel, Peter, and Charles C. Mann. 1994. *Material World: A Global Family Portrait*. San Francisco: Sierra Club Books.

Messner, Kate. 2015. *Up in the Garden and Down in the Dirt*. Illustrated by Christopher Silas Neal. San Francisco: Chronicle Books.

Millard, Glenda. 2012. *Isabella's Garden*. Illustrated by Rebecca Cool. Somerville, MA: Candlewick Press.

Mitchell, Joyce Slayton. 2005. *Crashed, Smashed, and Mashed: A Trip to Junkyard Heaven*. Photographs by Steven Borns. Berkeley, CA: Tricycle Press.

Mochizuki, Ken. 1993. *Baseball Saved Us*. Illustrated by Dom Lee. New York: Lee & Low.

Mulder, Michelle. 2014. *Every Last Drop: Bringing Clean Water Home*. Custer, WA: Orca Books.

Myller, Rolf. 1991. *How Big Is a Foot?* New York: Dell.

Nesbit, E. 2006. *Jack and the Beanstalk*. Illustrated by Matt Tavares. Cambridge, MA: Candlewick Press.

Noll, Sally. 1991. *That Bothered Kate*. New York: Greenwillow Books.

Norton, Mary. 1953. *The Borrowers*. Illustrated by Beth Krush and Joe Krush. New York: Harcourt, Brace & World.

Osborne, Mary Pope. 2005. *Kate and the Beanstalk*. Illustrated by Giselle Potter. New York: Aladdin Paperbacks.

Parnall, Peter. 1986. *Winter Barn*. New York: Macmillan.

Patent, Dorothy Hinshaw. 2008. *When the Wolves Returned: Restoring Nature's Balance in Yellowstone*. Illustrated by Dan Hartman and Cassie Hartman. New York: Walker.

Paterson, Katherine. 1977. *Bridge to Terabithia*. Illustrated by Donna Diamond. New York: T. Y. Crowell.

Paul, Miranda. 2015a. *One Plastic Bag: Isatou Ceesay and the Recycling Women of the Gambia*. Illustrated by Elizabeth Zunon. Minneapolis: Millbrook Press.

———. 2015b. *Water Is Water: A Book About the Water Cycle*. New York: Roaring Brook Press.

Paulsen, Gary. 1999. *Canoe Days*. Illustrated by Ruth Wright Paulsen. New York: Doubleday Books for Young Readers.

Peña, Matt de la. 2015. *Last Stop on Market Street*. Illustrated by Christian Robinson. New York: G.P. Putnam's Sons.

Peterson, Cris. 2010. *Seed Soil Sun: Earth's Recipe for Food*. Illustrated by David R. Lundquist. Honesdale, PA: Boyds Mills Press.

Pollak, Barbara. 2004. *Our Community Garden*. Hillsboro, OR: Beyond Words Publishing.

Posada, Mia. 2000. *Dandelions: Stars in the Grass*. Minneapolis: Carolrhoda Books.

———. 2007. *Guess What Is Growing Inside This Egg*. Minneapolis: Millbrook Press.

Prince, April Jones. 2005. *Twenty-one Elephants and Still Standing*. Illustrated by François Roca. Boston: Houghton Mifflin.

Rathmann, Peggy. 1995. *Officer Buckle and Gloria*. New York: G. P. Putnam's Sons.

Ratliff, Thomas M. 2010. *You Wouldn't Want to Work on the Brooklyn Bridge! An Enormous Project That Seemed Impossible*. Illustrated by Mark Bergin. New York: Franklin Watts.

Reich, Susanna. 2015. *Fab Four Friends: The Boys Who Became the Beatles*. Illustrated by Adam Gustavson. New York: Henry Holt.

Reid, Margarette S. 2011. *Lots and Lots of Coins*. Illustrated by True Kelley. New York: Dutton Children's Books.

Richards, Jean. 2002. *A Fruit Is a Suitcase for Seeds*. Illustrated by Anca Hariton. Brookfield, CT: Millbrook Press.

Riggs, Kate. 2009. *Golden Gate Bridge*. Mankato, MN: Creative Education.

Robbins, Ken. 2005. *Seeds*. New York: Atheneum Books for Young Readers.

Rocco, John. 2011. *Blackout*. New York: Disney/Hyperion Books.

Rockwell, Anne F. 1999. *Our Stars*. San Diego: Silver Whistle/Harcourt Brace.

———. 2016. *Let's Go to the Hardware Store*. Illustrated by Melissa Iwai. New York: Henry Holt.

Rosenstock, Barb. 2012. *The Camping Trip That Changed America: Theodore Roosevelt, John Muir, and Our National Parks*. Illustrated by Mordicai Gerstein. New York: Dial Books for Young Readers.

———. 2014a. *The Noisy Paint Box: The Colors and Sounds of Kandinsky's Abstract Art*. Illustrated by Mary GrandPré. New York: Knopf Books for Young Readers.

———. 2014b. *The Streak: How Joe DiMaggio Became America's Hero*. Illustrated by Terry Widener. Honesdale, PA: Calkins Creek.

Ruurs, Margriet. 2005. *My Librarian Is a Camel: How Books Are Brought to Children Around the World*. Honesdale, PA: Boyds Mills Press.

Rylant, Cynthia. 2000. *In November*. Illustrated by Jill Kastner. San Diego: Harcourt Brace.

Salas, Laura Purdie. 2014. *Water Can Be . . .* Illustrated by Violeta Dabija. Minneapolis: Millbrook.

Samworth, Kate. 2014. *Aviary Wonders Inc. Spring Catalog and Instruction Manual: Renewing the World's Bird Supply Since 2031.* Boston: Clarion Books.

Santat, Dan. 2016. *Are We There Yet?* Boston: Little, Brown.

Sayre, April Pulley. 2005. *Stars Beneath Your Bed: The Surprising Story of Dust.* Illustrated by Ann Jonas. New York: Greenwillow Books.

———. 2007. *Vulture View.* Illustrated by Steve Jenkins. New York: Henry Holt.

———. 2008. *Trout Are Made of Trees.* Illustrated by Kate Endle. Watertown, MA: Charlesbridge.

———. 2013. *Eat Like a Bear.* Illustrated by Steve Jenkins. New York: Henry Holt.

Schaefer, Lola M. 2000. *This Is the Sunflower.* Illustrated by Donald Crews. New York: Greenwillow Books.

———. 2006. *An Island Grows.* Illustrated by Cathie Felstead. New York: Greenwillow Books.

———. 2013. *Lifetime: The Amazing Numbers in Animal Lives.* Illustrated by Christopher Silas Neal. San Francisco: Chronicle Books.

Schwartz, David M. 1985. *How Much Is a Million?* Illustrated by Steven Kellogg. New York: Lothrop, Lee & Shepard Books.

Scieszka, Jon. 1989. *The True Story of the 3 Little Pigs.* Illustrated by Lane Smith. New York: Viking Penguin.

Seeger, Laura Vaccaro. 2007. *First the Egg.* New York: Roaring Brook Press.

Selznick, Brian. 2007. *The Invention of Hugo Cabret.* New York: Scholastic.

Sendak, Maurice. 1962. *Chicken Soup with Rice: A Book of Months.* New York: Harper & Row.

———. 1963. *Where the Wild Things Are.* New York: Harper & Row.

Seuss, Dr. 1954. *Horton Hears a Who!* New York: Random House.

Shannon, David. 2008. *Too Many Toys.* New York: Blue Sky Press.

Showers, Paul. 2001. *What Happens to a Hamburger?* Illustrated by Edward Miller. New York: HarperCollins.

Siddals, Mary McKenna. 2010. *Compost Stew: An A to Z Recipe for the Earth.* Illustrated by Ashley Wolff. New York: Dragonfly Books.

Sidman, Joyce. 2011. *Swirl by Swirl: Spirals in Nature.* Illustrated by Beth Krommes. Boston: Houghton Mifflin Harcourt.

Simon, Seymour. 1993. *Weather.* New York: HarperCollins.

———. 1999. *Tornadoes.* New York: Morrow Junior Books.

———. 2003a. *Hurricanes.* New York: HarperCollins.

———. 2003b. *The Moon.* New York: Simon & Schuster Books for Young Readers.

Sís, Peter. 2000. *Madlenka.* New York: Frances Foster Books.

Sisulu, Elinor. 1996. *The Day Gogo Went to Vote*. Illustrated by Sharon Wilson. Boston: Little, Brown.

Slobodkina, Esphyr. 1985. *Caps for Sale: A Tale of a Peddler, Some Monkeys, and Their Monkey Business*. New York: Harper & Row.

Smith, David J. 2002. *If the World Were a Village: A Book About the World's People*. Illustrated by Shelagh Armstrong. Toronto: Kids Can Press.

Snyder, Laurel. 2015. *Swan: The Life and Dance of Anna Pavlova*. Illustrated by Julie Morstad. San Francisco: Chronicle Books.

Soehlke-Lennert, Dorothee. 2015. *How Big Is Big? How Far Is Far?* Translated by Jen Metcalf. Illustrated by Jan Van Der Veken. Berlin: Die Gestalten Verlag.

Spinelli, Eileen. 1991. *Somebody Loves You, Mr. Hatch*. Illustrated by Paul Yalowitz. New York: Bradbury Press.

———. 2007. *Heat Wave*. Illustrated by Betsy Lewin. Orlando: Harcourt.

Steig, William. 1986. *Brave Irene*. New York: Farrar, Straus, and Giroux.

Stewart, Melissa. 2014. *Feathers: Not Just for Flying*. Illustrated by Sarah S. Brannen. Cambridge, MA: Charlesbridge.

Stewart, Sarah. 1997. *The Gardener*. Illustrated by David Small. New York: Farrar, Straus, and Giroux.

Stojic, Manya. 2000. *Rain*. New York: Crown.

Stone, Tanya Lee. 2008. *Elizabeth Leads the Way: Elizabeth Cady Stanton and the Right to Vote*. Illustrated by Rebecca Gibbon. New York: Henry Holt.

Sturges, Philemon. 1998. *Bridges Are to Cross*. Illustrated by Giles Laroche. New York: G. P. Putnam's Sons.

Sullivan, Martha. 2015. *If You Love Honey: Nature's Connections*. Illustrated by Cathy Morrison. Nevada City, CA: Dawn Publications.

Swift, Jonathan. 1976. *Gulliver's Travels*. New York: St. Martin's Press.

Taback, Simms. 1999. *Joseph Had a Little Overcoat*. New York: Viking.

Tanaka, Shelley. 2001. *Attack on Pearl Harbor: The True Story of the Day America Entered World War II*. Illustrated by David Craig. New York: Hyperion Books for Children.

Tolstoy, Aleksey Nikolayevich. 1968. *The Great Big Enormous Turnip*. Illustrated by Helen Oxenbury. New York: Franklin Watts.

Uhlberg, Myron. 2011. *A Storm Called Katrina*. Illustrated by Colin Bootman. Atlanta: Peachtree.

Van Allsburg, Chris. 1981. *Jumanji*. Boston: Houghton Mifflin.

VanDerwater, Amy Ludwig. 2013. *Forest Has a Song: Poems*. Illustrated by Robbin Gourley. Boston: Clarion Books.

———. 2016. *Every Day Birds*. Illustrated by Dylan Metrano. New York: Orchard Books.

Viorst, Judith. 1972. *Alexander and the Terrible, Horrible, No Good, Very Bad Day*. Illustrated by Ray Cruz. New York: Atheneum.

Waddell, Martin. 1992. *Farmer Duck*. Illustrated by Helen Oxenbury. Cambridge, MA: Candlewick Press.

Wahl, Jan. 2011. *The Art Collector*. Illustrated by Rosalinde Bonnet. Watertown, MA: Charlesbridge.

Ward, Jennifer. 2009. *The Busy Tree*. Illustrated by Lisa Falkenstern. New York: Marshall Cavendish.

———. 2014. *Mama Built a Little Nest*. Illustrated by Steve Jenkins. New York: Beach Lane Books.

Watson, Renée. 2010. *A Place Where Hurricanes Happen*. Illustrated by Shadra Strickland. New York: Random House.

Wells, Robert E. 2012. *Why Do Elephants Need the Sun?* Chicago: Albert Whitman & Co.

Whelan, Gloria. 2014. *Queen Victoria's Bathing Machine*. Illustrated by Nancy Carpenter. New York: Simon & Schuster.

White, E. B. 2012. *Charlotte's Web*. Illustrated by Garth Williams. New York: HarperCollins.

Wick, Walter. 1997. *A Drop of Water: A Book of Science and Wonder*. New York: Scholastic.

Wiesner, David. 1988. *Free Fall*. New York: Lothrop, Lee & Shepard Books.

———. 2006. *Flotsam*. New York: Clarion Books.

Willems, Mo. 2004. *Knuffle Bunny: A Cautionary Tale*. New York: Hyperion.

Williams, Vera B. 1981. *Three Days on a River in a Red Canoe*. New York: Greenwillow Books.

———. 2007. *A Chair for My Mother*. New York: Greenwillow Books.

Winter, Jeanette. 1992. *Klara's New World*. New York: A. A. Knopf.

Winter, Jonah. 2012. *Just Behave, Pablo Picasso!* Illustrated by Kevin Hawkes. New York: Arthur A. Levine Books.

Wolff, Virginia Euwer. 1998. *Bat 6*. New York: Scholastic.

Wood, Audrey. 1982. *Quick as a Cricket*. Illustrated by Don Wood. New York: Child's Play (International).

Woodson, Jacqueline. 2012. *Each Kindness*. Illustrated by Earl B. Lewis. New York: Nancy Paulsen Books.

Yolen, Jane. 1992. *Letting Swift River Go*. Illustrated by Barbara Cooney. Boston: Little, Brown.

Yolen, Jane, and Heidi E. Y. Stemple. 1999. *The Mary Celeste: An Unsolved Mystery from History*. Illustrated by Roger Roth. New York: Simon & Schuster Books for Young Readers.

———. 2015. *You Nest Here with Me*. Illustrated by Melissa Sweet. Honesdale, PA: Boyds Mills Press.